ADVANCE PRAISE FOR
THAT DAY AND WHAT CAME AFTER

Author Rebecca Daniels and I have a lot in common, We both found and married our husbands a bit later in life. We both had our marriage stories cut short in an instant by death, and we were both widowed by cardiac arrest. *That Day and What Came After* is the book I wanted and desperately needed to read back in July 2011, when my husband, Don, left for work one ordinary Wednesday and never came home.

Back when my world collapsed and I felt completely alone and terrified, I needed the soothing and validating words that Daniels provides as she gently and lovingly walks us through what it's like to be suddenly widowed. I needed to know, by reading this book, that I would get through this, and that I was normal in feeling changed forever by the experience.

In addition to her grief story, Rebecca gives us a beautiful glimpse into the love story between her and Skip, and as readers, we almost feel as if we are losing him too. As a writer, Rebecca has a way of making the words flow so that reading them feels less like an effort and more like floating or being guided along.

As both a fellow widow and, most recently, a grief counselor, I will be recommending this book to future clients and those I meet in the widowed community. Nothing can bring back those we love who have died, but as Rebecca demonstrates in this memoir, the love lives on forever, as we each find beautiful ways to create purpose and meaning out of that which makes little sense. The message is clear and certain: Love is the only thing that matters.

—KELLEY LYNN, CERTIFIED GRIEF COUNSELOR, VIRAL TED TALK SPEAKER, AND AUTHOR OF *MY HUSBAND IS NOT A RAINBOW: THE BRUTALLY AWFUL, HILARIOUS TRUTH ABOUT LIFE, LOVE, GRIEF, AND LOSS*

Rebecca Daniels' *That Day and What Came After: Finding and Losing the Love of My Life in Six Short Years* lovingly guides us through her experience of the unexpected death of her husband from sudden cardiac arrest.

This memoir, rich with details and imagery from her marriage with Skip, comes together to craft a work of genuine love that delights in their relationship and extends that joy to its readers. As a culture we tend to discuss death so infrequently that Rebecca Daniels' unflinching and brave decision to wade headlong into that subject is like a balm for those of us looking for catharsis and to make sense of the unimaginable.

A beautiful portrait of love, loss, and grief; a roadmap for travelers who find themselves on this unfortunate path, and a practical guide for helping them walk through this experience, *That Day and What Came After* is an indispensable read for anyone looking to not just "get over" the death of a loved one, but transmute the experience into something more meaningful . . . something more human. I will be recommending *That Day and What Came After* to my clients who are struggling to come to grips with, and ultimately integrate, an experience as jarring and unmooring as losing a loved one.

—JAY SEFTON, LICENSED MENTAL HEALTH COUNSELOR

That Day and What Came After is a beautiful love story from beginning to end. Rebecca Daniels invites us into her story of falling in love later in life, her husband's sudden death, and ten years of evolving grief.

Daniels' memoir is a helpful companion for people who are grieving, especially for women who have lost their husbands suddenly. While each person's love and loss is different, this memoir serves as a reminder that they are not alone. It is helpful for people in the beginning stages of grief when it is hard to concentrate, and they may feel numb and brain dead. It is also a good read for people who need a counter voice to those who expect them to be "over their grief," as a reminder that mourning continues in different manners with ever evolving forms of grief as well as new rhythms and patterns of resilience.

This memoir is a helpful grief companion, especially for persons who are spiritual but may not be a part of a formal religion. She wrestles honestly with her own questions about life after death. Daniels does not provide answers but creates a place for honest and raw questions that the reader may contemplate or discuss with a pastoral or spiritual leader, or a counselor.

This is not a self-help book, or a compendium of answers, but an honest and compelling story of ongoing grief, which is not afraid to ask tough questions. Daniels describes some practical things she experienced that helped her through the agony of grief, which range from having a professional grief counselor to a timer on the light switches, so she didn't come home to a dark empty house.

In addition to being a companion narrative for people who are grieving, I recommend Daniels' memoir to people who want to be a better friend or family member to someone who has lost a beloved spouse. It gives the reader an understanding of what someone might be experiencing in their grief.

Since the memoir was written looking back, it takes us through the grief experience from the initial shock of the trauma through the years of loss and the resilience and hope of going on through new stages of grief.

—REV. DR. THERESA MASON, RETIRED UNITED METHODIST MINISTER, FORMER PASTOR OF CHURCHES IN CALIFORNIA AND NEBRASKA, AND FORMER CHAPLAIN AT HAMLINE UNIVERSITY IN MINNESOTA.

That Day and What Came After is a moving story of a love found later in life and lost too soon. In this memoir, Rebecca contemplates deeper questions and chronicles navigating the minutiae of day-to-day life after losing her beloved partner. Heartbreak and loneliness are tempered by found family and precious memories. By turns sorrowful, hopeful, and reflective.

—NATALIE PINTER, AUTHOR OF *THE FRAGILE KEEPERS*

THAT DAY AND WHAT CAME AFTER

FINDING AND LOSING THE LOVE OF MY LIFE IN SIX SHORT YEARS

REBECCA DANIELS

SUNBURY
PRESS
Mechanicsburg, PA USA

Published by Sunbury Press, Inc.
Mechanicsburg, PA USA

SUNBURY
P R E S S ®
www.sunburypress.com

For information about special discounts for bulk purchases, please contact Sunbury Press Orders Dept. at (855) 338-8359 or orders@sunburypress.com.

To request one of our authors for speaking engagements or book signings, please contact Sunbury Press Publicity Dept. at publicity@sunburypress.com.

FIRST SUNBURY PRESS EDITION: May 2024

Set in Adobe Garamond Pro | Interior design by Crystal Devine | Cover by Lawrence Knorr | Edited by Sarah Peachey.

Publisher's Cataloging-in-Publication Data
Names: Daniels, Rebecca, author.
Title: That day and what came after : finding and losing the love of my life in six short years / Rebecca Daniels.
Description: Second trade paperback edition. | Mechanicsburg, PA : Sunbury Press, 2024.
Summary: What if you came home and found your husband dead in his favorite chair? This memoir explores the author's experience of the unexpected death of her husband from sudden cardiac arrest a mere three months after his doctors pronounced him hale and healthy. The author shares details of the couple's later-in-life courtship and marriage as well as experiences she has had along the grieving road since becoming a widow.
Identifiers: ISBN : 979-8-88819-204-7 (paperback) | ISBN : 979-8-88819-205-4 (ePub).
Subjects: BIOGRAPHY & AUTOBIOGRAPHY / Memoirs | FAMILY & RELATIONSHIPS / Death, Grief, Bereavement | FAMILY & RELATIONSHIPS / Marriage & Long-Term Relationships.

Designed in the USA
0 1 1 2 3 5 8 13 21 34 55

For the Love of Books!

To
SKIP STOUGHTON
(7 November 1947 – 9 October 2010),

❧❧❧

my beloved and my friend,
whose unconditional love while we were together
gave me the courage and strength to write about
his loss when the unimaginable happened
and his big heart stopped unexpectedly.
His memory sustains me always.

OTHER BOOKS BY
REBECCA DANIELS

Finding Sisters:
How One Adoptee Used DNA Testing and Determination to
Uncover Family Secrets and Find Her Birth Family
(Sunbury Press, 2021)

Keeping the Lights on for Ike:
Daily Life of a Utilities Engineer at AFHQ in Europe During
WWII; or, What to Say in Letters Home When You're
Not Allowed to Write about the War
(Sunbury Press, 2019)

Women Stage Directors Speak:
Exploring the Influence of Gender on Their Work
(McFarland & Company, 2000)

CONTENTS

CONTENTS

PREFACE

AS A CULTURE, we in the United States tend not to talk much about death or grieving, especially within our families, and my family was no exception. As a young teen, I remember seeing my mom take the call about her father's death with a slight quiver of her lip and tightening of her jaw as she worked hard to hold in her feelings in front of her daughter. Mom was raised by a mother with strict Victorian standards; "A lady never shows her feelings" was Gran's mantra. And when my father died just three weeks after his fifty-seventh birthday due to medical complications following what should have been a routine ulcer surgery, Mom was not inclined to talk about her grief, though it was clear to the rest of the family that she was in deep shock and struggling to maintain some semblance of a balanced demeanor, even as her world had been turned upside down.

So, at age twenty-three, after five years of living independently hundreds of miles from where I grew up—at college, during summer breaks, and for the year after graduation—I found myself living at home again to be sure our mother, in her mid-fifties at the time, would be okay on her own. My brother was an undergrad at a small liberal arts university in a nearby city, so he was able to visit now and then, but as a varsity track athlete, he had regular training to attend to in addition to his college coursework.

For the first few weeks, I counted Mom's pills each day because her doctor had given her some strong sedatives to ease her shock and grief, and she had voiced thoughts about not being able to live without Dad. But these melodramatic moments started to wane, and after several more months, her spirit showed increasing signs of returning to something approaching her normal demeanor, though it was obvious, even to my youthful self, that her life would never be the same again. Even then, she wouldn't talk about her feelings, not to me, and perhaps not even to her sisters or her close friends. She had never been forthcoming about her emotions, even when things were going well, so it's no surprise that she kept her grief and grieving to herself. She hated "being a bother" to anyone. Further, our culture encourages, even expects us, to keep our grief out of the public view, and my introverted mom was happy to oblige. She kept it all inside.

Though I missed my dad, I was young and eager to get on with my own life, so when I felt she was no longer in need of "supervision" (such as it was), I decided to return to where I'd been living before Dad's hospitalization and death. Mom and I never talked about grieving again, though she did start talking about Dad now and then, and we would look at his slides whenever I visited (he had been an avid photographer). I presumed seeing these images was her way of engaging the memories that sustained her in the more than three decades she lived on her own after his death. So, while she never delivered any direct advice about how to live as a widow, she modeled for me the possibility that one could lose the love of one's life, survive that devastating experience, and find a new life living alone that seemed, to all who knew her, to be one of contentment, even peace.

I first heard the term "new normal" in the context of grief counseling in the weeks after Skip died. It was ubiquitous in that milieu, though it also seemed to be used in a variety of other instances, such as after 9/11, after the financial crisis of 2008, and even about life after the pandemic of the early 2020s. More than anything else, and regardless of whatever specific incident might set the need for a new normal in motion, to me, the term meant finding a new way to live a reasonable life after a world-shattering experience, whether it be personal, national, or worldwide. This book is my story about the long and winding grieving road I took toward finding my own new normal after my beloved husband died.

Mom predeceased Skip by four years, so she was not available to talk to when I needed her advice the most. In her absence, I looked for written stories from women like me who had lost their spouses, but there weren't many. Much of what I found was focused on self-help strategies for grievers of all kinds, or books focused on the more spiritual/religious side of dealing with death or loss. But what I wanted—needed, in fact—was to hear stories from others who had been down this road before me. I wanted to know what happened in their daily lives as they tried to put their world back together in a way that, even if it didn't make sense at first, was tolerable, even healing. This is why I decided to share my own story of grief and grieving, of accepting the mantle of widowhood, however reluctantly, and of learning how to live again and even to thrive in my new normal. This is not a book I ever expected to write, but I hope my story can be helpful to someone who finds herself in a similar place one day and is looking to hear from others who've gone down this grieving road before.

ACKNOWLEDGMENTS

MUCH GRATITUDE goes to my women's writing group led by the ever-encouraging and always-astute Jane Roy Brown, including the various and changing members of this group (Mollie Babize, Cate Bosarth, Rosemary Caine, Annie Cheatham, Carole Fuller, Fran Henry, Jeanne Johns, Becca King, Mariel Kinsey, Marilyn McArthur, Sherrill Redmon, and Karen Spindel) who between them heard all of the chapters (and some of them twice) as they were originally developed between the summer of 2017 and the end of 2018, and who offered excellent feedback and encouragement all along the way.

Thanks also to my former employer, St. Lawrence University, who provided a generous emeritus faculty grant to allow me to hire the editorial expertise of Jane Roy Brown to help with conceptualizing and structuring the final organization of the disparate writings that make up this memoir.

Heartfelt thanks as well to the fantastic team at Sunbury Press, especially Lawrence Knorr, founder and CEO, for his belief in the importance of this book and his attention to the details of getting it in front of the reading public. I was pleased and privileged to work with Sarah Peachey as my editor as well as with book designer, Crystal Devine, and cover designer, Lawrence Knorr.

Thanks to special friends and neighbors, Zachary Dorsey and Diane Exoo, who were there for me in the immediate weeks after my loss in everyday ways, who kept me from going off the deep end by dropping by for a walk or inviting me over for a drink, to share a meal, or other "normal" activities at a time when I was feeling anything but normal. Thanks to longtime friend Mary Mears Haskell for flying across the country to help me confront cleaning out Skip's side of the closet months after his death.

Thanks to Rebecca Rivers and her Northern Light Yoga Studio, who helped me put my body back together after grief had crushed it, so that my spirit could return to me. And thanks to other good friends and family members, too many to name, who fed me for that first month when I could barely taste my food much less have any interest in cooking, who gave words of advice and/or encouragement as I put my life back together after the shattering of my world, who helped me pack up my house and prepare for a move to a new community, and in general who made it possible for me to resume something resembling a normal life.

Special thanks to my brother and sister-in-law, Toby Daniels and Debbie McKeown-Daniels, who shared my grief and helped me purchase a beautiful memory tree to plant in the place where Skip used to have his wonderful veggie garden.

A posthumous thanks to my parents, Mary and Alec Daniels, both excellent amateur photographers who nurtured in me the love of documenting life with photos. Those images of my life with Skip and all the joy those memories bring to me, have been my solace during my journey toward that elusive new normal.

And finally, very special thanks to my immediate family: stepdaughter Kensey, son-in-law Tim, and grandchildren Maren and Trenton Batchelder, who have offered unconditional support, love, and strength throughout my journey along the grieving road—even as they traveled the same road along with me—and who provide me with joy and a sense of home and belonging in my new community in the aftermath of the unthinkable.

CHAPTER ONE

THAT DAY

SATURDAY, OCTOBER 9, 2010, dawned bright and sunny. The list of yard winterizing tasks Skip and I wanted to accomplish was long. We were planning to go down to visit the grandkids during my mid-semester break, so we wanted to get things done while we had the chance. The weather looked to be warm and perfect for working outside, but first I had a meeting to go to. It was unusual to have an academic meeting on a Saturday, but this was the first gathering of a special task force of faculty and administrators handpicked by the university president from all divisions of campus, a meeting I couldn't say no to, nor did I want to. So Skip and I talked about which jobs we needed to do first that afternoon, made a short grocery list of things I would pick up on my way home from campus, said our usual "see you laters" and "love yous" with a quick kiss, and Skip headed upstairs for a shower as I set off for the morning's gathering.

Our job on this new task force was to start work on a vision statement for the future of St. Lawrence University in the next decade, which we would present to the trustees at their February meeting. To get everyone to agree to a weekend meeting, participants had been promised a civilized start time—9 A.M. for coffee and muffins—followed by discussion from 9:30 A.M. to noon, with lunch immediately after the meeting was over. Our campus food service always put on a terrific spread for presidential events, so we were all planning to stay for what promised to be a nice meal as our reward for bringing our ideas for the future of the institution to the table on our day off. I had served as the faculty liaison to the

3

architects for the recent arts center renovation project, and I had chaired the professional standards committee recently (the first woman to do so), so I knew why I'd been asked to participate and was eager to discover who else had been picked for this endeavor. Among the two dozen or so faces around the horseshoe of tables when I arrived, I was heartened to see a number of people I liked and respected and with whom I worked well, but frankly, I don't remember much about the meeting or the luncheon. Only what came after.

When I came in through our side door to the sunroom with my groceries, the image I encountered seemed normal at first glance. Skip was in his usual recliner, bathed in prismatic sunlight from the nearby beveled glass window. The Cartoon Network was playing but muted on the TV, and it looked like he must have snoozed out after his lunch, which was not unusual. There was a partial glass of seltzer on the table beside him and an apple with one big bite taken lying in his lap, where he must have dropped it as he dozed off. But when I called his name, he didn't wake as usual, and there was something peculiar about the angle of his jaw, like it had unhinged at one corner, showing a section of back teeth I hadn't seen before when he slept, even if his mouth was ajar while snoring. I pushed this image from my consciousness as one might push away a nightmare upon waking, but I was too late: it was burned onto the back of my eyelids for a very long time afterward. "Honey, wake up," I called again, sharper and louder, but still he didn't rouse, so I dropped the groceries on a chair and tried to shake him awake to no avail. He'd had a couple of alarming low sugar moments in the past couple of years due to his type 2 diabetes, so the cool clamminess of his neck when I touched it hinted this might be the problem today, but his face and arms were warm from the sun, so I didn't know what to think or do next. But I knew I needed to call for help.

The 911 operator was calming and helpful. After dispatching the EMTs to my house, she directed me to get him out of the chair and onto the floor in case his airways were blocked from his position in the chair, but I wasn't strong enough to move him. I must have started to sound panicked because the next thing she asked me was whether there was a friend or neighbor she could call for me. My next-door neighbor's number was one of the very few I had memorized because we called each other so often. I rattled off the number, and the 911 dispatcher kept talking to me until my friend Diane arrived in just a matter of minutes. The ambulance and the EMTs were only a couple of minutes behind her. They got Skip out of the recliner and onto the floor, then went to work to figure out why he was unresponsive. Diane drew me into the nearby living room and onto a small couch where we were out of their way but could still see what was happening. One of the EMTs pulled out a manual device that looked like a soft football with a mouthpiece at one end (I later learned this was called an Ambu bag) and tried to help him breathe while the second EMT performed CPR. I remember hearing Diane whispering, "Did you see that? His chest is moving; he must be breathing," but I couldn't tell whether he was breathing, or the bag was breathing for him. The EMTs got Skip on a stretcher and had him out the door very quickly, and Diane ran next door to get her car while I sat in a daze, trying to grasp what was happening.

On the drive to the hospital, I remember calling my stepdaughter, Kensey, to tell her what had happened and that I'd call her again when I got to the hospital. She and I were no strangers to her dad being in the hospital, since he had a minor stroke followed by an emergency carotid endarterectomy three years before, and he'd had surgery for thyroid cancer two years ago, but this was his first medical emergency in a long time. In fact, his diabetes was well controlled with meds, he was now considered cancer-free, and all his doctors had pronounced him in tip-top shape at his annual exams within the past three months. Diane had been my driver on one of those other occasions, and she tried to lighten my apprehension by reminding me how well things had turned out the last time we took this drive to the hospital. When we got to the ER entrance, a nurse bustled us into a side waiting room instead of bringing us right into the patient area. "Your husband was just brought in, but I need to check with the doctor before bringing you inside." Those words gave me a bad feeling, but I tried to keep my thoughts upbeat. After all, he'd been in this situation before and all had been well, but in the previous incident, he had been awake and joking by the time we got to the ER.

After just a few minutes, the nurse returned and asked us to follow her. She walked very close beside me, with Diane behind us, and as
we entered the patient area, she whispered in my ear, "Sorry, honey, he
didn't make it." I don't know if she thought she was softening the blow
that would be coming from the doctor in a few moments, or if she just
wanted to beat the doctor to the punch, but my heart lurched. I don't
remember the words the doctor used to tell me my husband was dead,
because the nurse's whispered comment was still ringing in my ears, but
then I was led into the room where my handsome husband was laid out
on the bed. Another nurse, not the one who had murmured in my ear in
the hallway, was standing next to me by the bed saying, with an edge of
sadness in her admiration, "What an attractive man!" And he was.

In death, he had lost the vivacity and animation that made him such
a delightful companion and wonderful host to our friends and family,
but he hadn't yet lost his color and looked for all the world like he was
sleeping. That sense of peace in him was one of the details that brought
me some solace in the days, weeks, and months to come. The doctor was
sure that he had felt no pain as he passed out and then away. They left
me alone with him, and I spent some time memorizing every detail of
his face, running my fingers through his silky silver hair, and feeling what
residual warmth remained in his big hand as I clutched it one last time.
I kissed him goodbye, and it wasn't the increasing coolness of his touch
that was hard to bear, it was the lack of responsiveness in those lips that
had always been so eager that broke my heart.

Feeling numb and not knowing what to do next, I took my last look
and emerged from the room where his body lay, feeling more than a
little lost. The doctor assured me that Skip had most likely died from
sudden cardiac arrest and may have been dead already when I arrived
home, though his body had still been warm from the sunlight streaming
in the window. There was no evidence in his demeanor nor reported
by the EMTs at the house that would suggest that there had been any
trauma in his death. His heart had just stopped, and whatever reaction
he had experienced would have included a feeling of drowsiness before
he lost consciousness. A small blessing for him. Not so much for me. The
hospital wanted to know where to deliver the body, and with a jolt of

Zachary admitted later that he didn't have any memories of me hunched or stooped or curled into a ball . . . I was just gone—off in my mind and my memories and the sedatives and wherever else Skip's death led me. He said, "I just remember that being a thing—our powerful Rebecca wasn't shrunk down or reduced at all . . . she just went away for a good long while." Once I was alone and could let go of my self-imposed constraints, I discovered by instinct what keening meant. I wept and wailed and sobbed—deep, guttural sounds—as sorrow overtook me, and I rocked and shook until I was exhausted. Even so, I couldn't imagine how I might be able to sleep, so I took another of the pills the doctor had given me, which allowed me to fall into a restless sleep for a few hours. When I woke feeling muzzy and cold at 5 A.M., I curled toward where Skip should have been in the bed, but finding it empty, I started fully awake. Surely the day before had been a horrible dream . . . but where was he? Why wasn't he here with me where he belonged? Then the details of the previous day came back with shocking clarity. He was gone. Forever.

When one experiences trauma—such as the shock of finding your husband dead only weeks after all his physicians had pronounced him hearty and healthy—linear thinking goes out the window. The next several days are a blur, but I have a few sharp recollections of things that happened. The first thing I did after that bitter awakening was to decide that the important people in our lives already knew what had happened, and to admit that I didn't have the stamina for any more notification phone calls to more distant friends, so I posted Skip's picture on Facebook with the following caption: "The love of my life: Harold Webster [Skip] Stoughton, 11/7/47 - 10/9/10. I'll miss you, Daddy Cat . . ." Then I messaged Kensey to see how she was doing and started to pack for the trip I was about to take. Diane drove me from Canton through the Adirondacks to North Creek, where another family member took over, driving me the last hour to Fort Edward to meet up with Kensey and Tim. Normally, this was a drive I enjoyed, and it was nearing peak autumn leaf season, so I'm sure it was a beautiful ride, though I have no memory of the trip. I do have a vague awareness of staying at Kensey's cousin's house for the night (though I'm not even sure which cousin it was) and then going to the funeral home the next day to choose a coffin

This image, taken just months before it happened, is the one I posted on Facebook to announce Skip's death. It also became the image on his funeral card.

(plain, inexpensive, but not bottom of the line—we thought Skip would have approved) and to make the rest of the arrangements for the funeral the following day (not too much Bible talk, please). Kensey did most of the talking but always made sure I agreed with her choices, and I was so proud of how in control she seemed. It reminded me of how, at age twenty-three, I had taken charge when my own father had died because my mom had retreated into herself, and I wondered if I was repeating history, but I couldn't muster the energy to do anything different. There was a photo board of images of Skip at various ages at the funeral home, and I know I had something to do with it, but I can't envision how I managed that, though perhaps I had the wherewithal to send the digital files to the funeral director after my early morning awakening, since he managed to come up with a framed 8x10 color photo I had taken of Skip on Kensey and Tim's deck five months earlier when we had come down for our grandson's birth.

At the funeral, I remember feeling overwhelmed, though not surprised, by how many people were there that I didn't know. After all, this was where Skip had grown up and later taught in the school system for many years. I'm sure I was wooden and distant because that was how I was holding the grief at bay, but Kensey and Gloria, Skip's mother, flanked me in the reception line and during the service, which gave me some comfort. The next thing I remember was standing in the funeral home parking lot by myself, feeling lost and bereft, wondering where everyone had gone, then being rescued by Kensey's maternal Aunt Sue, who was outraged that the pallbearers and funeral director had taken Gloria in the hearse with the coffin for the drive to the cemetery but had left me behind. Sue and her husband drove me to the grave, and they told me Kensey and Tim had gone to check on their kids, a three-and-a-half-year-old toddler and a five-month-old infant, but they would soon be meeting us at the cemetery for the graveside service.

After the burial, I found myself at the wake Gloria had arranged at a local social club on the Hudson River, where the family had been members for years. Zachary and our friends from Canton, who had made the drive down, stuck close to me as the gathering got larger and louder because of the generous refreshments and open bar, all paid for by Gloria. I have two distinct memories from that event, and both of them felt like gut punches at a time when I had no strength to resist the blows. Old friends of Skip's, who had known his first wife and may not have realized that he had remarried after her death, were talking in animated tones about Skip and Shirley being reunited in heaven. When I heard that, I must have gasped or faltered in some way, because my Canton friends surrounded me and moved me out of earshot of the hometown group's drunken reminiscences. Not too long after that encounter, it was time for my friends from up north to start their long drive home. After I bid them farewell, my ever-astute son-in-law noticed that I was struggling, and offered to take me back to where we were staying since he needed to check on the kids. Tim wanted to let Kensey grieve with her old friends and extended family for as long as she needed and was as uncomfortable in this large crowd as I was.

After saying good night to Gloria and Kensey, we made our way outside, where a second shock slammed me. My sister-in-law, hammered and intense, came running after us, berating me for taking the pills she'd heard the doctor had given me to help deal with my anxiety and grief. While I stood rooted in the parking lot, speechless and shaky, she lectured me about how addictive clonazepam was, and said no matter how calming or helpful the drug might seem to be, it was dangerous and should be discarded without delay. With sensitive care and gentleness, Tim guided her back into the party while I got into the car, trembling and on the verge of a meltdown. I knew that drinking was how she was coping with Skip's death, and using her professional knowledge as a nurse was her way of trying to take care of me, but between the two events, I was on a knife's edge of hysteria and didn't want to slide over into a breakdown. I didn't want to inflict that on Tim since he was already being so helpful, so I focused on trying to stabilize my breathing, holding the sobs at bay until he returned, and we headed in silence to our lodging.

I don't remember anything else from the day of the funeral, or how we said goodbye to Gloria, or the two-hour drive to Kensey and Tim's the following morning, but another vivid memory from those few days hit us all as we entered their condo. There were bright images of prismatic light all over the wall in their living room! I had told Kensey about how Skip's body had been bathed in similar light from the beveled glass window when I found him, and seeing that light, we both felt he was here with us, that his spirit—which neither of us had felt at the funeral, or at the graveside, or at the wake—had followed us home. We could see what was creating the effect (a sunbeam hitting a CD jewel case edge just so), but that didn't stop us from associating that rainbow light with Skip's memory from that point forward, no matter where or when we encountered what we always called "Skip's prisms." In fact, the window that created that first light effect has come with me to my new home in retirement, and when our grandchildren were younger and the sun

This is the antique window that created prismatic light on Skip in our sunroom as he slumped, unresponsive, in his favorite chair.

shone through it, creating rainbow patterns on the dining room and living room walls and floor, one or both of them would often cry out, "Papa's here!"

CHAPTER TWO

WHAT CAME AFTER

WHATEVER THE HELL it turns out to be, the new normal waits for no woman. It doesn't care if you are ready; it's there whether you like it or not, and it drags you along, kicking and screaming, though not always out loud. You can pretend it's not happening while you're in hyperdrive, dealing with the immediate aftermath—the funeral, the wake, the burial—but it's part of your life now, no matter how much you don't want it to be there. I don't remember a thing about how I got ferried home from Kensey and Tim's after being with them for four days after Skip's funeral, though I know the six-hour drive involved them, a brother-in-law, Kensey's maternal Aunt Sue and her husband, and my friend Diane for the last leg. I imagine Di, known to her friends as "Wolf Mama" for her fierce protectiveness of everyone she cared about, would have made sure I had everything I needed and wouldn't have left me alone until she was sure I would be okay. I do remember I had a hard time sleeping that night, and for many nights thereafter, without taking more of those pills my sister-in-law had warned me about.

My first cogent memory of my new aloneness was of coming downstairs that first morning to a cold house, which bothered me more than usual, even though I had always been the one who got up first and turned on the heat during the "old" normal. Being alone in the house made the cold seem more challenging somehow, so the first thing I did was call my furnace guy to ask about getting a programmable thermostat so the house could be warm when I got up. I pulled some light timers I had used when I lived alone out of storage, so there would be no darkness downstairs when I came down alone, especially as the long winter gloom approached. Next, in an attempt to resume my usual routines in hopes they would bring me some solace, I started a load of laundry, much of it Skip's, but found myself just standing in front of the washer taking in his smell on each item of clothing before I could put it in the washer. After a long while, I put in the soap and turned the washer on, and this action did bring me some small comfort because I could pretend that he was away somewhere and would be home soon. However, I also set aside a couple of my favorite shirts of his without washing them, keeping them for several weeks, inhaling the scent of him whenever I was feeling overwhelmed by loneliness.

While I was going about these household routines in hopes of bringing back a sense of normalcy to my life, I discovered that "widow brain," as I later heard it referred to in my counseling sessions and online grieving groups, was definitely a thing. It's a kind of grief-induced amnesia as our brain tries to protect us from the pain of a deep loss. Ever the consummate multitasker in the past, I could no longer hold even the simplest of thoughts in my head for any length of time. I imagine it must be a preview of what dementia might feel like. I'd go into a room and forget why I was there or even how I got there in the first place. If I was talking to someone on the phone, I'd pause, sometimes in the middle of a sentence, not knowing what to say next, or even what I had just said. And I started running into furniture I'd been navigating with ease for years, which gave me bruises on my hips and legs, sometimes my arms or shoulders, and the look of someone who was being battered by an imaginary assailant. One day, I missed the last step coming downstairs because I wasn't paying attention and landed so heavily on my left leg that the jolt went all the way up to my shoulder. I'm lucky I didn't take a full tumble. After another cold and nearly sleepless night, I started spooning his pillow and inhaling the scent of it to help me relax and feel warmer. Soon, I started narrating my life to myself as it was unfolding during the day—"time to switch the laundry," "maybe I should make some tea," "let's see what's in the fridge for lunch"—in hopes that it would keep me from forgetting what I was doing as well as to keep the house from being so quiet all the time.

The second full day home meant my first day back on campus. One of my introductory classes had been taken over by another instructor, and other colleagues had taken over the play rehearsals until I felt I could return, which left me with only one class to deal with on my own. The students were all upper-level theatre majors, mostly seniors, and the small class was on the verge of starting their final directing projects and working independently during class hours, which meant they wouldn't need much from me on a regular basis, even under normal conditions. I told them that I would be there for them as much as I could under the circumstances but that I had no idea what would be possible for me since I was medicated because of shock and deep grief. I'm sure they could tell about the meds, because I wasn't my usual animated self in class; they had to take the initiative to ask for help, because I wasn't going to audit their work during the rehearsal process as I had planned to do. They were eager to be helpful by working on their own, and most of them were more than capable of doing it all without much intervention from me at this point in their academic careers. That brief visit to class and a short visit to the arts office to pick up my mail was all the energy I could muster for one day, so I went home and just sat in Skip's chair for the rest of the afternoon, basking in the same beautiful light that had bathed his body when I first found him. I might even have slept a bit in the warmth and comfort of those prisms in a chair that still smelled like my husband.

The next day, reality came crashing in on me, and I could no longer tell myself that Skip's death had been a bad dream from which I would awaken any moment: his official death certificate came in the mail. After talking with our lawyer about next steps, I realized I had to start looking in Skip's desk for all our financial account information. It took an extra anti-anxiety pill to allow me to sit there without trembling and crying so I could accomplish what was needed. Over the next few days there were lots of necessary tasks: visiting the Social Security office to file for death benefits (I was appalled to discover that the "benefit" in 2010 was only $255, though his funeral and burial would cost me $10,000!), taking all of Skip's maintenance meds to the local hospital for proper disposal, getting my monthly allergy shot (almost but not quite late), visiting the grief counselor for the first time, and the one enjoyable task—visiting an animal shelter. In those first few days home alone, I decided I really needed another warm body in my life, and while there would never be a replacement for my "heater man," a new pet was something I wanted and needed right away.

Our old cat, Jasper, had died the previous spring, and we'd decided to wait until the following year to get a new one. Skip, who claimed he wasn't a cat person, had developed such a strong boy-bond with that sweet longhaired tabby that when we decided the time had come to put Jasper to sleep because his cancer could no longer be managed, Skip couldn't stop crying and had to be comforted by the vet tech while I held the cat and the vet administered the fatal injection. This emotional attachment had earned him the nickname of "Daddy Cat" long before Jasper grew ill. Following the cat's death, Skip had insisted he was much too sad to think about a new pet so soon, but now that he was gone, I knew I couldn't, and wouldn't, wait for spring. I did stay true to the other detail of our plan, though. I wouldn't get just any cat. We had agreed to look for an adult ginger cat to adopt, and since I knew they were almost always male, I decided that I would name this new cat Webster in Skip's honor. Though no one had ever called him anything but Skip his entire life, his legal name had been Harold Webster Stoughton III. In hindsight it seems remarkable, but within a few days, a little online searching of regional shelter websites during a couple of my sleepless nights helped me find an adult ginger cat available for adoption only twenty miles away.

When I first approached this big orange fluffball, a surrender who had been unimaginatively named Garfield by his previous owners, the cat immediately sat up tall on the utility shelf where he'd been snoozing, put his paws around my neck, head-butted my chin, purred, and climbed into my arms. I had found my guy! I didn't realize just how fortuitous a discovery it was until after I got him home, though. From the very first night, he lay on my chest, purring, as I sobbed. Once my breathing normalized and the tears stopped, Webster would move down to the foot of the bed, and when I rolled to my side to clutch Skip's pillow to my chest, the cat snuggled in the small of my back, helping to keep me warm as I slept.

Among the things that fascinated Webster in his new home were the prisms on the floor of the sunroom.

My grief counseling sessions, which started soon after I returned home from the funeral, all seem to blur, one into the next, but the most valuable lesson I gained from those conversations was to "give voice to my sorrow," as the counselor encouraged. So, because I wasn't always ready to talk during civilized hours for visiting, and sometimes I didn't know I needed to talk until it was too late to call someone, I took to joining online widow's groups for occasional interaction with others struggling with the same issues. I didn't last too long in the online groups, though. The two things that drove me away were the super-Christian widowed people, who insisted that our spouse's deaths were all part of God's plan, that those we had lost were "in a better place," and that we all needed to accept Jesus in our life, so our troubles would be over. They weren't the majority of voices, but they certainly were the loudest and most insistent. I didn't need proselytizing—I needed uncritical allies for the grief journey. Many widowed people were also convinced they would be seeing their beloveds again in heaven, and they were holding out desperate hope for that reunion. In spite of not having strong religious convictions about heaven or an afterlife, that issue became a conundrum for me because I'd married a widower who wed the love of his life in his twenties and lost her to liver failure nearly three decades later. And yet he opened his heart to me in this life after she was gone. But if there is reunion in the afterlife, those folks who were consoling themselves at the wake with the Skip-and-Shirley-together-again-in-heaven narrative were right. So where did that leave me? It was a persistent spiritual problem for me for many weeks after Skip's death, and I was looking for a way to manage the paradox. I tried to open that conversation in a couple of different groups but gave up after a few tries because folks who were clinging hard to that consoling narrative didn't want to imagine any other possible outcome for their own stories, so they rejected mine. I did find a couple of non-widowed friends willing to engage in that conversation, and one gave me a helpful concept from her own spiritual belief system by insisting that if there was an afterlife, in that place love would expand to be greater than our current limited human understanding of the concept, and there would be no competition, no either/or to deal with. This belief helped me to stop torturing myself so often with worry about a comparison between myself and Skip's first wife.

In those early weeks, I started journaling with focused intensity—entries were raw and vulnerable, both furious and bereft, addressed directly to Skip—as well as posting a modified version of my personal grief journey more fit for public consumption on Facebook, and the conversations those posts initiated became a kind of lifeline for me that autumn. In fact, I did so much online posting that a Communication Studies colleague in the department suggested I write an article or book about online grieving since, to her knowledge, no one had ever written about it before. But by the time I could write more than the occasional short post or bleak and often maudlin fragments in my private journal, it was too late; others had started to write those kinds of articles. Frankly, I wasn't that interested in doing it in the first place. To me, the words were an outlet for my own feelings and kept me from imploding as I plodded along this uneven path toward that fucking new normal to which I was now trying to adapt.

Early November brought three milestone moments for me. First, the play I had been directing when Skip died opened to general acclaim and large audiences. I was so proud of the work everyone had done since I had abandoned them. Zachary had been serving as my production dramaturg and had taken over the direction with the help of another good friend and colleague when it became evident that I could not continue. At Zachary's suggestion, we had dedicated the production to Skip's memory, and he had written a beautiful tribute for the program. Second, a few days after opening night would have been Skip's sixty-third birthday, so a few close friends gathered that evening to toast "the bartender" with his favorite cocktails, making it the first of many "should have beens" to appear in my journal entries and Facebook posts. It also marked my growing awareness of how these anniversaries, large and small, can hijack your emotions when you least expect it. Just days after Skip's birthday was the anniversary of a month since his death, which felt at once both ages ago and just yesterday.

The third moment that started complicating my life and put my relationship with a close friend in a complex conflict with my family bonds was when I discovered that both my mother-in-law and my stepdaughter had, unbeknownst to me, contacted two of the financial houses where Skip and I had our retirement investments, notifying them of his death and inquiring about account information. This resulted in me not being able to access the account information online for myself, even though I had account details and passwords. A phone conversation straightened things out, but my friend was incensed on my behalf and, in her hyper-protective mode, insisted that they were more greedy than grief-stricken, that she had seen this behavior many times in her legal practice. She felt it meant that neither of these women trusted me to do the right thing, whatever that might be, with those financial assets, even though I held all the power, being the beneficiary and the joint account holder. This set me to fretting about my ongoing relationship with the family and with our grandchildren. Would the latest addition to the family—me—be the first one jettisoned now that my connecting link had been lost? To my relief, Kensey's Aunt Sue helped me see that because of temperament and some past experiences, both Kensey and her grandmother tended to focus on specific, controllable details (like business and finances) as a way of trying to dampen their own heartache, and

Kensey and I were able to work out the issues of inheritance over time. However, these new fears shook me to my core, and I realized that I had to stop confiding in Diane about estate details if I wanted to maintain any relationship with Skip's mother and daughter. But it also reassured me that none of this was really about me, but about how these family members were coping with their own deep grief.

Though the funeral had been more than a month ago, mid-November was when I had planned a local memorial in our home for all the Canton friends who could not make the long drive to Fort Edward for the family funeral, burial, and wake. For the memorial, I had invited about fifty local friends to our house, many of whom had also been at our commitment ceremony five years earlier. I also invited a dozen family members from out of town, though most had attended the other funeral, and I was more or less certain none of them would make the trip north. In the invitation to this event, I promised to have Skip's favorite cocktail, a Manhattan, available to anyone who wanted one, and I asked everyone to bring some food to share. I also previewed the evening:

> We will toast him and tell stories about our memories of him. Feel free to bring readings if you don't want to speak off the cuff. Feel free not to speak at all but just to join the celebration. Feel free to play music or sing songs in his honor. Feel free to stay as short or as long a time as you like.

The event brought a full house and overflowed into the kitchen and dining rooms as friends crowded into our rarely used formal living room. After an opening toast "To Skip" from everyone, and a lovely musical interlude from a colleague, the sharing began. Diane read a poem about death that had been part of the first funeral, and Ann Marie read a compilation of comments from friends and relatives all over the country that she had also read at the funeral. Another friend, who shared Skip's devotion to the Red Sox, read his own "top ten Red Sox memories" about growing up a Sox fan in Yankee territory. Then, to end the planned part of the program, Ann Marie read a beautiful tribute from Kensey, who had been unable to attend in person because her husband, Tim, couldn't get away. Kensey shared several sweet memories of her dad and addressed the audience directly at one point:

> I could blab on and on about what an amazing man he was. I also feel fairly confident in the fact that I don't need to do that because if you have come to this gathering, then you knew my father, and by his sheer nature you knew that the world was a far better place for having had him in it.

Then she closed with one last memory and these words: "To me, he was the picture of class, honor, integrity, and respect, and you can't ask for a better dad than that."

Then I opened it up to the group for any other comments they wanted to add, the highlight of which was Skip's good friend, Gregg, sharing his story about how they had been "grounded" by me for a year over their bad behavior a couple of winters ago. Skip had been helping Gregg with the bookkeeping and taxes for his landscaping business, and to celebrate the completion of some phase of the tax planning, they had gone out for lunch, where they started drinking. Neither Ann Marie nor I had any idea where they were for several long hours and had started to worry about what might have befallen them when Gregg helped Skip up our outside stairs, both of them blotto and laughing like a couple of teenagers. Skip had a cut on his cheek, the result of a faceplant on the ice in the bar parking lot, but they had made it home otherwise unscathed. In both relief and anger, I hollered that they were forbidden to go out drinking together for a long, long, long, long time. Since Gregg was a neighbor, they could drink at either house any time they wanted, but I didn't want either of them behind the wheel if they were drinking. Ever. The funniest part of the story was that the next day, Gregg was furious that he had a terrible hangover, but Skip, nearly twice his age, didn't, likely because Gregg was drinking Coke with his Captain Morgan, but Skip was having his rum straight. His story made everyone laugh, but Zachary told me later that Gregg had been weeping in the kitchen during the rest of the memorial because he was missing his friend so much. I ended this segment of sharing with my own statement about Skip, which

I had written in advance because I didn't trust my emotions enough to improvise in public:

> In most of my adult relationships, love had been contingent, conditional, but Skip's love was different. When he loved, he loved unconditionally: me, his family, his friends, and most especially his daughter, Kensey, her husband, Tim, and his grandchildren, Maren and Trenton. He was taken away from all of us much too soon, and his loving presence will remain with us forever in our memories.

Then, on the edge of tears but never quite tipping over, I read the poem about love and true partnership that had been read at our commitment ceremony. The evening closed with another colleague playing his saxophone and singing a jazz-inflected gospel song called "Just a Little While to Stay Here" about approaching the end of one's life. As he was leaving, a department colleague asked me if I knew what had been wrong with the evening. Astonished, I simply shook my head. He said, "Skip should have been here; he would have loved this." He wasn't the only one who spoke those words during the evening, but my feeling was that what was wrong was the fact that we had to have this party at all. This memorial marked the end of my ongoing ability to cocoon in the comforting but unrealistic denial of his death. I wrote in my grief journal the next morning, "I think I'll now have to admit that you are gone, that this is not some extended nightmare from which I will wake up one day."

When I called Kensey the next afternoon to tell her all the details about the memorial, she told me that Maren, then three-and-a-half, was still talking regularly to her Papa (Skip) on her plastic toy phone, something she had started to do when I was with them in the days after the funeral, nearly a month before. Kensey was starting to suspect that Maren had figured out that saying she was "sad about Papa" got her hugs or kisses, so she might be working that angle for extra cuddles. But Maren was also trying to figure out what to do with her own sense of the loss of her beloved grandfather. The more often I talked with Kensey, the more I realized that anything she had said or done in the early days

Maren and her Papa shared a special sympatico, and she talked to him on her toy phone for several months after his death.

of mourning that ignited my worries about my future within the family had been part of her own struggle with grief and had little to do with me, though it may in some ways have reflected her own fears about the possibility of losing me next.

We decided that we wanted our Thanksgiving rituals to change this year, even if only temporarily. She would call Aunt Sue to implore that she host the festivities this year. Though I was not emotionally ready yet for sorting through all of Skip's things, and the big purge of his closets and drawers was still months away, we decided to give away a small number of things right away to a few who had been close to him. We agreed that all the Red Sox memorabilia and Beach Boys albums should go to his brother Mark, who was also an avid fan, that his cigars and cigar paraphernalia should go to Gregg since the two of them had been known to share stogie moments, and we gave Zachary a brown corduroy cap that Skip had worn in college and which was featured in one of the images from the funeral display, because we knew that he had loved that particular photo. Each of these gestures meant a lot to the men who had loved him, each in different ways: brother, buddy and role model, and father surrogate. It's hard for men to grieve openly in our society, and I believe they each acquired some comfort from receiving Skip's "gifts." I was regretting that my mom had never been comfortable talking to me about her own grieving after my dad died. He was just fifty-seven and she fifty-six, and Skip and I were just five years older than my parents had been, yet I had never thought to ask my mom about her experience in detail when I was younger. Probably because I thought it would never, ever happen to me.

CHAPTER THREE

THE BARTENDER
IS A KEEPER

My first marriage lasted only eight years. By the time my divorce was finalized in the winter of 1984, my ex-husband and I had been living apart for almost three years, and both of us were seeing other people. That spring, I entered into a new live-in situation that lasted another three years before it went bust, as many rebound relationships do. For the next several years, there was no significant romance in my life. In fact, there were only two brief affairs: one with an old high school flame (and it didn't work any better the second time around) and a short-term fling with a gregarious salesman who traveled a lot and eventually fell in love with a flight attendant. In the decade that followed, I got comfortable living alone and with no significant other in my life. It was a period of celibacy and self-satisfaction, sexually speaking, which didn't actually bother me, though I did miss companionship. However, being on my own was a nice change from the previous decade of fraught and unreliable relationships.

It was the summer of 2003 when friends decided I'd been alone long enough and convinced me to put a profile on an online dating site. Thus began my online dating odyssey. I started with a ninety-day introductory membership to Match.com by creating my profile and spending some time exploring the various online profiles of men in my age range and geographical location. I had read all the warnings about screening the people one meets online with care at first, so all encounters started with a few getting-to-know-you conversations using email, and in-person meetings took place on neutral ground at lunchtime. I did have a few expressions of interest that were all about quick sex, so I eliminated those right out of the gate. It took some time before I started to meet what one can only call "prospects" in person. And there were only a handful of those that got beyond the initial email stage.

Notable among the one-date wonders was an extremely tall (6'7" to be exact), thin, and sweaty-palmed fellow who had been quite articulate and interesting in email conversations but who had almost nothing to say in person other than to tell me in great detail about the meds he took for his lactose intolerance and how he had discovered the precise number of supplements to take in order to be able to eat dairy products without problems, all this as he pulled out his pills so he could have cheese on his sandwich. Next was an obese pear-shaped fellow with a handsome face, piercing eyes, and an affable and intelligent demeanor who confessed after less than fifteen minutes that he was smitten and wanted to see me again soon but admitted he wasn't interested at all in a friendship if it wasn't going to lead to sex. The pièce de résistance was the one I call the "date from hell." He was a flushed and balding redhead with slurred speech and a slight stagger, even before lunch was served (during which he kept on drinking). He wanted to walk around after lunch, and pulled me into a shop with expensive Alpine sweaters in the window, insisting in his outdoor voice that I would buy a sweater, but only if the manager would lower the price. I turned and left with a quick apology to the clerk, and once we were outside, he grabbed me and tried to kiss me. Due to his drunken unsteadiness, I was able to shove my gloved hand between his mouth and mine. If he had been a little less drunk, I might have been more fearful, but he could barely stay upright, so I was sure I could get away from him with little trouble.

"I'm done with you," I said as I pushed him away, "don't contact me again," and headed toward my car.

"Bitch," he shouted after me but didn't follow, and for days he sent me emails in all caps about how horrible I had been to him and what a cunt I was. He was more pathetic than scary, but he definitely put me off another in-person meeting with a new man any time soon.

When it came time to renew my trial membership, I let it lapse, but out of disinterest or laziness, I didn't bother taking down my profile. For the uninitiated, anyone can put a profile on Match.com for free as well as browse other profiles, and the first way to contact others on the site is through something called a "wink," which means a quick click to let someone know you were interested. However, if you want to talk to that person via email, you have to have a paid membership. So with a lapsed membership, I would get a wink from a man now and then, check out his profile, and then decide it wasn't worth re-upping my membership to find out more about him.

Almost a year after my foray into the world of Match.com, I got a wink from a man who had a very interesting profile, the kind I would have responded to when I had my membership. He was a retired high school social studies teacher, someone with similar tastes in music and shared political views, a widower who had recently moved to northern New York from the southern Adirondacks. I winked back, realizing that it meant nothing since I was not inclined to renew my membership for one handsome former teacher who might or might not be a good match. Silence followed, and I had almost forgotten about his wink when I got an email at my work address. It was polite and said that he was looking for the Rebecca who had a profile on Match.com, but since he hadn't paid his dues, he was unable to contact her through the site. I realized that in my naïveté, I had put enough information in my profile to make it possible for someone to find me if they tried hard enough. Teaching theatre in a small liberal arts college in northern New York left only a few places to check out, and I hadn't used a clever alias for my profile, just my first name. Friends joked later that it might have been considered stalking, except that, in this case, the end result was positive. He was friendly and straightforward, saying if I wasn't the person to please excuse his presumption, but if I was that Rebecca whose profile he'd seen on Match.com, he'd like to get to know me.

It didn't take long for me to decide. What did I have to lose? He knew the same things about me that he might have discovered if we were conversing on the dating site, but because the memory of that date from hell was still fresh in my mind, I kept things in the email phase longer than before. This man's name was Skip, a childhood nickname that he had kept into adulthood because he didn't like his given first name, Harold. My dad had been a Harold who also hated his first name and used his middle name with family and friends, so I understood. Skip and I wrote back and forth on a regular basis for several weeks before finally agreeing to meet in person in late July 2004. We arranged a time and place to meet for lunch, and he told me what car he drove, which I thought was odd but didn't give it much more thought.

The appointed day and time arrived, and I waited for him in the restaurant lobby for about thirty minutes before heading home in a fury. I tossed off an angry email as soon as I got home. How could he be so rude! It was about an hour before I got a long, thoughtful reply to my angry message. He had been waiting for me in his car, he said, and thought he might have seen me leave the restaurant without stopping to look around the parking lot. He apologized for mixing up the meeting details due to his nerves. How could he imagine that I'd know the difference between one black car and another, and why would he expect me to cruise the parking lot looking for him, I countered, thinking this might be another candidate for a date from hell. But he asked if I would give him another chance. We could meet at the same restaurant, but in the lobby this time. Perhaps it was intuition at work, but I decided to give him that second chance.

Our first lunch date was low-key and pleasurable. He was tall, with a deep voice, silver hair that showed signs of once having been dark brown, and hazel eyes that stayed focused on me with interest without being creepy. We had no trouble keeping the far-ranging conversation going for more than an hour, though the fact that he had a cocktail with lunch gave me a minor twinge. I had a good friend who was on the verge of leaving her marriage because of her husband's alcoholism, and I was in no mood to put myself in a similar situation. So I wrote to him that evening, explaining that even though I had enjoyed meeting him, if he couldn't meet with me without needing alcohol, we couldn't meet again. He replied right away that he'd been anxious because of his previous gaffe about where to meet and said he would be happy to abstain next time. He knew about alcoholism, he admitted; his first wife had died of alcohol-related liver disease, but he had no trouble not drinking. Would I please give him another chance? How about Saturday?

"I'm sorry," I said, "I've got plans that day to go down to my favorite garden store to bring home several bags of a special mulch that I can't get anywhere else."

"That sounds great," he replied, "I love to garden. Maybe I could come along and help you carry the mulch bags?"

I didn't have a comeback for that unexpected reply, and besides, it would be nice to have someone's help, so I said, "Sure, why not?" I thought doing something different than a typical date would be a good test to see if this guy would fit into my lifestyle or not. There's no doubt he was appealing. And every interaction we'd had so far—except for that weird misunderstanding about the first meeting—had been quite comfortable and engaging. He was easy to talk to and easy on the eyes, so I thought this second date, however unorthodox, might help me decide whether or not I would continue to see him.

That Saturday, he drove to my house and we got in my car together to head down to the nursery. I am a much better driver than a passenger, and I had no interest in having him be in full control of the driving at this point, but that didn't cause him any problems. About twenty miles into the fifty-mile drive through rural northern New York, as we were admiring a small farm with a large cobalt blue silo on the side of the road, my car stopped running with no warning. There was no coughing of the engine, no jerking as we slid to a stop, no sounds or smells that would have caused us to worry, just a sudden quitting of the engine, which forced me to pull over a few hundred yards past a small cluster of houses. There was no hope of restarting the engine; it wouldn't turn over at all, and the three houses on one side and the small farm on the other side of the road were the only signs of civilization in the midst of the sprawling fields we had just been driving through. Skip didn't seem too freaked out about it, didn't insist on checking under the hood, and seemed content to let me take the lead in whatever our next move might be. As I flipped on the flashers, I explained I had an up-to-date AAA membership, so we needed to find a phone because neither of us had a cell phone. I suggested that I would walk over to the nearest house to use the phone, and asked

A view of our "breakdown" spot from the downhill side. My car stopped just before the road started to head downhill past the silo.

him to stay with the car in case someone drove by to offer help. It took knocking on doors at all three houses before I found someone at home and willing to let me use their phone to call the emergency road services dispatcher, who was quick to schedule a tow truck to come help us. As we waited for rescue, Skip and I continued to talk with ease about nothing important, the kind of getting-to-know-you talk that we had shared at our lunch. What kind of music do you listen to? What good books have you read recently? Where's the rest of your family? Tell me about your last garden . . . and so on. It was during that conversation that I learned he had been the owner and chief bartender of a small Adirondack hotel for six years from the late seventies to the mid-eighties, one of his many professional identities through the years.

When the tow truck arrived, I realized that we were going to have problems. The AAA dispatcher had been miles away in central New York and didn't understand the roads and towns in the northern part of the state at all, so instead of sending a truck from Gouverneur, several miles straight down the highway, she had arranged for a tow from a garage in a tiny town called Russell, closer as the crow flies but a more complicated drive on back country roads. But it was too late to complain. The driver ascertained that there was nothing he could do to get the car going again; the problem was a broken timing belt that would need to be replaced, so we'd need to tow the car back to his home garage for repairs. The driver was terse and uninterested in conversation, so we all crammed into the pickup cab and made the silent drive back to Russell, where he deposited us and my car at the repair shop.

The most important question we had for the mechanic who confirmed the initial diagnosis for us was whether or not they had the necessary part in stock. They didn't; it would have to be ordered and wouldn't arrive until Monday. This being midday on Saturday, we would need a loaner car, but the garage was too small to have any available. We would have to find a way to get home after leaving the car with them. Before tackling the transportation dilemma, we decided to look for a place to have lunch.

On Main Street in Russell, the only street as far as we could tell, there were no restaurants, but besides the general store, where we could have bought some groceries, there was one small place offering pizza by the slice, so we opted for pizza over packaged snacks. Turns out it was frozen pizza for take-out only. Most local customers must have taken the slices home to cook, but we asked if they could heat the slices for us since we were stranded at the moment. They heated them in a microwave and served them to us on paper plates with paper towels for napkins, which we took to a bench on the sidewalk in front of the store. They also let us use their phone, so once we had eaten I started calling for rescue. After several fruitless calls, I contacted a friend who, as a North Country native, knew where Russell was and how to get there but wouldn't be able to set out for another fifteen or twenty minutes, and it would take her half an hour to get there from her place. I agreed. So, Skip and I spent another hour sitting on the bench in the middle of a tiny country town, exchanging pleasantries. To my delight, there were no tensions, and we were even able to sit comfortably in companionable silence when we ran out of topics for conversation. Once we were delivered back to my house, I suggested we have dinner somewhere in town but made it clear that sharing the evening would not lead to spending the night at my place. He seemed fine with that decision but said he would like to see me again and hoped he could help me with the gardening stuff when my car was finally fixed.

Our next date was dinner at his home, a beautiful riverfront lot in a small town a forty-five-minute drive from my place, where he served shrimp scampi in lemon sauce, a fresh salad, and his own homemade French bread, complete with an excellent white wine. Neither my ex-husband nor my former live-in partner had had much interest in cooking, and after nearly a decade of living alone, I was no longer a regular cook, so it was a wonderful surprise to spend time with someone who liked cooking and wanted to woo me with food. But still I resisted his sexual advances. There was no doubt that he was ready to take things to the next level, and I was starting to see that there was a possible future with this guy. But I wasn't going to sleep with him. Not yet. I suppose it was fear of intimacy after close to fifteen years of being on my own. It's not always easy to navigate relationships, and mine had not been very successful in the past. Was I really ready to share my life with someone again? I found this guy attractive and tempting, but something held me back for a little while longer. To his credit, he didn't push things. He made it clear that he was attracted to me and would like to sleep with me, but he was never angry when I stopped things from going that far and said he'd wait until I was sure I was ready.

This went on throughout August, and he patiently kept returning for visits of all kinds, most of them involving hours of conversation. Slowly and surely, we were getting to know each other better. I told him all about my psychologically abusive husband, and about the live-in boyfriend with two young children who had hedged his bets with a woman on the side for the duration of our three years together. And I was learning more about his first wife, Shirley, an intelligent and creative high-functioning alcoholic who had died three years before we met. He had been in one other relationship since her death. In fact, that relationship was why he had moved to northern New York in the first place. He had wanted to sell the house he had shared with Shirley for so many years because there were too many painful memories, and he also had wanted to test out a new long-distance relationship he had been enjoying for several months. Unfortunately for him (and fortunately for me), she kicked him to the curb about six months after he had moved to the area and three months before he saw my online profile.

When September rolled around, I decided I was ready to let the budding romance turn sexual. But I was going to do it in my house and on my terms. I invited him for dinner, and after dinner we had a nice bonfire in my patio fire pit. When the conversation turned into kissing and the kissing got more impassioned, I asked him if he would like to spend the night. He was ready and had been hoping for this invitation for a while. In his eagerness, he bonked his head—hard—on the door frame of the steep and narrow stairs to my bedroom, but he was able to laugh it off. Afterward, we found our bodies fit together quite nicely. I can't say the sex between us was earth shattering, but it was pleasant and, to my surprise, easy for me even though it had been almost a decade since I'd invited a man into my bed and my body.

The problem came when it was finally time to sleep. My cats didn't want him in the bed, especially Sophie, the queen female who ran the household and had been my primary companion since I first arrived in Canton. I hadn't been without a cat or two for any length of time in the past two decades, so it was important that he accept their presence, but it was more important for them to accept this stranger into the house. Sophie didn't scratch Skip or hiss, but she didn't give him any ground, either. She was going to sleep right next to me on my right side as she always did, and she didn't care whether this big man wanted to be there or not. She kept burrowing between us no matter how often we tried to push her away. So, then we tried Skip on my left. Jasper, the younger cat who hadn't been around for as long as Sophie, was unhappy at first but didn't put up much resistance and let Skip cuddle up to my left side, then curled in behind him. So, there we were, sandwiched in by two large adult longhaired cats. Skip didn't seem to be upset by the feline drama. In fact, he seemed both bemused and amused. Though it might have seemed like a minor detail to a non-cat person, this was a major test. I had decided that if Skip didn't like the cats or wouldn't allow them to sleep near him, that I wouldn't be able to do so, either. But he passed the cat test and became quite fond of both of them, though Jasper was his special buddy.

In mid-October, during my mid-semester four-day-weekend break, we took our first romantic getaway trip, to Quebec City. Though I didn't

history of Major League Baseball. So, when the Sox won game four to keep the Yankees from sweeping the playoffs, it was beyond exciting. Our lovemaking was more passionate than usual that night. Then came games five and six, and against the odds, the Red Sox kept winning. When it came to the seventh game, the tension in front of the TV was intense, and I started to get into the spirit of being a serious Red Sox fan. I was even getting used to Skip's stubble. We were both ecstatic when the Sox beat the Yanks in that seventh game, earning the right to play in the World Series that year. That was when the talk of the Curse of the Bambino really began, and I started to understand some of the Red Sox mythology as well as the history of the rivalry between the two teams. I had no idea that Babe Ruth had been traded to the Yankees in 1919, which had (in the minds of many fans, Skip included) led to an eighty-six-year drought, during which the Red Sox, previously one of the most successful franchises in Major League Baseball, had failed to win another World Series. This was their chance to reclaim their former glory.

So, the Sox were going to the World Series, Skip's facial hair continued to grow, and I learned a whole lot about professional baseball from my new sweetheart. I hate to think that the relationship might have foundered if I hadn't been able to show honest interest in one of his major passions. As luck would have it, I did love and understand the game of baseball, having played it, and played it well, as a youth and been quite frustrated by the lack of opportunities for girl baseball players when growing up. Watching the World Series was actually less dramatic than watching the playoffs, because the Sox dominated from the beginning and never lost a single game. Once they had won the World Series and finally broken the Curse of the Bambino, Skip declared, only somewhat tongue-in-cheek, that I was his good luck charm and he was going to have to keep me around for future seasons. And I was happy to be kept, which meant it was time to start planning for the holidays and deciding how to introduce each other to our families.

CHAPTER FOUR

MEETING THE STOUGHTON CLAN

AFTER A PLEASANT three-hour Sunday drive south through the Adirondacks, where a bit of color was lingering here and there, even in mid-November, we came out of the mountains to find ourselves on the main street of the bucolic small town of Hudson Falls, New York. We turned onto a series of tree-named streets and pulled into the driveway of a charming one-story house with a partial brick front and a small, well-kept yard under a large maple tree, now nearly denuded of leaves. There were already several cars parked on the street nearby, and I realized this was it; I was about to meet Skip's mom and other family members for the first time. I went from feeling relaxed to on edge in the space of a few accelerating heartbeats. It had been fifteen years since my last serious relationship, and with both my ex-husband and the live-in partner who followed, we had little or no engagement with extended family members, so this was a completely foreign experience. Skip must have noticed the change in my breathing as we walked to the front door toward the family party his mom was hosting in my honor. As we stepped onto the low front stoop, he squeezed my hand with a quick smile and assured me everything would be just fine. So, I smiled back at my new love, squared my shoulders, lifted my chin, and got ready to play my part.

Gloria's short hair was as curly and carefully coiffed as her oldest son's was straight and shaggy, though both sported the same striking shade of silver. Though she was short and he was tall, their facial resemblance was unmistakable. The rest of the family members waiting in Gloria's cozy living room were much less distinctive. Though Skip had given me a family preview on our drive down, it took me months to keep all the names and relationships straight, and on this particular day I simply smiled at everyone, trying to remember who they were and how they fit into the jigsaw puzzle of the Stoughton clan. My first reaction was relief that they were all dressed casually, as Skip had assured me they would be, so visually, at least, I fit right in. Gloria was a no-nonsense hostess, and as soon as she'd introduced me to the half dozen people sitting around the living room, she hauled Skip off to the kitchen to help her mix drinks (he was obviously her preferred bartender), and she started shuttling platters of finger food to the dining room, which left me alone in a room full of folks I'd never met. As I watched the only familiar face disappear into the back of the small house, my heart rate, which had calmed when we first entered due to Gloria's pleasant greeting, started to accelerate again, and my palms got sweaty all of a sudden. Here it comes: the moment of reckoning. But instead of the expected grilling—where was I from? how did we meet? what did I do?—I heard:

"That Denais, she's always late. . . ."

"Poor Scott. I heard he had to take an extra job because she just quit hers."

"Oh, I've heard she refuses to work full time, anyway. . . ."

"You know she won't eat anything and always complains that no one ever serves anything she can eat."

"I know. She'll bring special food for Shea, too, as if she and her daughter are too good for Gloria's cooking."

It took me a few minutes to absorb the fact that the women in the room seemed more interested in complaining about someone who wasn't there than getting to know me, which was ostensibly the purpose for the party. This was both a relief, because it took me off the hot seat, and a puzzlement. The only thing I knew about Denais was that she was the second wife of Skip's younger brother, Scott. I couldn't identify who was complaining about what just yet, but there were several voices involved, and as soon as the conversation turned in this direction, Skip's nephew escaped to join his uncle in making drinks in the kitchen, leaving me in a room full of women that I didn't know, bitching about another woman I hadn't met yet.

I was curious about this Denais person, but I must admit that my immediate worry continued to be for myself. "Oh, dear," I thought, "if this is what they have to say about the most recent newcomer to the family when she's not around, what will they have to say about me, another newcomer, once the party's over?"

I knew Shirley had been an integral member of this clan for nearly thirty years until her death three-and-a-half years prior, and it's hard to compete with the beloved dead. It took me weeks to realize it wasn't about Denais being the newest family member, but more because she was disliked for the way the other women—who I eventually came to realize were Skip's younger sister, her two daughters, her daughter-in-law, and Skip's youngest brother's two stepdaughters from his first marriage—how they all believed she took advantage of Scott's good nature for her own selfish needs. They also seemed to imagine that she was faking a medical condition, and they didn't think that eating the wrong food really could give her and her daughter the problems she complained about. Not one of them blamed Scott in any way for the family's late arrival or the supposed medical problems, and when he, Denais, their eight-year-old daughter, and Scott's teenage daughter from his first marriage finally arrived, everyone greeted the group with what looked to this stranger like cheerful enthusiasm. It was as if the previous complaints had never been voiced, and I realized that I might never truly understand what the women in this family thought about me.

Gloria presided over a party that, on the surface, seemed quite congenial and was more about catching up with Skip; meeting me was simply the excuse that made visiting with him possible. Now and then, I'd hear lowered voices mention Shirley, which didn't help me relax in their company. Even though nothing overt was said, and there was not much I could do about it, I still felt like I was being compared to her throughout the afternoon, and I started to wonder if this would be my future if I became part of this family. However, I was also starting to see that Skip, as well as being the oldest, was the favored son who could do no wrong, so even though the whispering was irritating, I started to worry less about what they thought of me. After all, if he chose me they would likely agree that I was acceptable, and Gloria, the most important voice in the room, had already made it clear that she liked me, just by being inclusive and solicitous of my comfort throughout the afternoon and evening.

As the party went on, I noticed that the Stoughton clan liked their liquor, especially younger brother, Scott, who got lively and loquacious after a few drinks and regaled us with stories about his experiences in clown college in his youth, as well as stories about what was happening with the juvenile offenders he worked with through the county corrections system. I was relieved not to be the star of the show, so I sat back and enjoyed the group energy while trying to identify and remember each person as they added to the conversation.

I found myself warming to Scott. I could see why Skip loved his little brother so much. Perhaps his combination of bravado and vulnerability was why the other women in the family were all inclined to want to protect him from his dour and, according to them, manipulative wife, though I had no reason that day or ever to perceive Denais as anything other than quiet, even shy in a crowd, and someone who picked at her food and didn't seem to have much of a party appetite. I was later to learn that both she and her daughter, Shea, had tested positive for celiac disease, that Denais was careful about their diet, and that the condition was more real and more serious than the rest of the women in the family were willing to admit.

When the crowd had dispersed, and after the leftovers had been put away, the dishwasher set to running, and Gloria was out of her hostess mode, I had a chance to get to know her better while the three of us shared a nightcap before bed. Family history was important to her, and she was pleased that on our way to her place, Skip had taken me by the house in Fort Edward where the Stoughton kids had grown up and Gloria had lived until Skip's dad died suddenly nearly twenty years before. Skip had explained to me that the town had once been the third most populous town in the Northeast, after Boston and New York, during the French and Indian War of the mid-eighteenth century, admitting that early American history had been one of his favorite subjects to teach when he was a high school social studies teacher. The house was a nondescript, low-slung ranch on a side street with thick woods in the back, and Skip hinted that plenty of youthful hijinks had taken place in those woods, though he didn't give many details. Due to a couple of miscarriages suffered by his mom, Skip had been an only child for his first seven years, and he was about twelve when the family, now with three more children, had moved into that house, which his folks built in 1959.

Skip also told his mom that he had taken me by the raised ranch near the old Stoughton family home where he and Shirley had lived before her death, grousing that the new owners didn't seem to have as much interest in the garden as he had, and insisting that it looked much nicer when he was in charge of the yard. He had also taken me by the Fort Edward Town Hall, a boxy, two-story brick building with lots of windows, where Gloria had worked as the Town Clerk for many years until her retirement more than a decade earlier. She enjoyed hearing about this pre-party tour, and talking about it had put me in mind of the time in my life when I was a teenager and my grandmother lived within walking distance of our house as had Skip's own. I had fond memories of Thanksgiving gatherings at Gran and Grandad's place, where all four of their daughters and families came for an annual celebration. Until today, I hadn't been to a similar family event for close to forty years. It felt good, and a wave of nostalgia and a sense of missing my own mom, who was three thousand miles away, hit me as we chatted into the evening with Gloria.

My immediate impression of Gloria's forthrightness was reinforced as our conversations continued, and I started to see similarities between her and my own mother, also someone who didn't care for crowds but braved them when necessary, who took refuge in mundane household details when faced with a group, and who rarely pulled her punches when asked her opinion about anything. Right from the beginning, I liked Gloria. I also understood that, like my own mother, she would never be physically or verbally affectionate with me, though I did get the sense that she approved of Skip's choice and would defend it, if needed. She confided that several folks, as they were leaving the party, told her they thought I looked and seemed a lot like Shirley, which Gloria perceived as a compliment. This surprised me because the only image I'd ever seen of Shirley was a wedding photo on Gloria's sideboard. I didn't see any physical similarities between the tiny, dark-haired woman with a pixie face smiling at the camera and my much more solid and substantial Nordic-looking self, but Gloria was adamant that the facial similarities were real. Though I struggled with the comparison at first, worrying about what difference this might make in my developing relationship with Skip, I nodded and smiled at Gloria, having decided it was not such a bad thing to be likened favorably to a man's deceased first wife, especially when the marriage had been long and stable. And the comparison did seem to give me a leg up in his mother's affections, such as they were.

When it was time to turn in, Gloria ushered us into her tiny guest room and pulled the trundle bed out from under the daybed. She didn't pull the trundle up all the way, and she had made each single mattress up with separate linens, but when we were alone, Skip pulled the trundle up level with the other bed. However, the bar in the center and the separate linens on each piece made it very clear that this contraption would not convert to a double bed, and there would be no snuggling tonight. I was exhausted and overstimulated, but after we turned out the bedside light, I grilled him: Was he sure things had gone well? What did his mom mean by the comparison to Shirley? How could he tell whether his relatives liked me? As we whispered into the night, Skip enthused in his warm, deep voice that he thought the party and our visit with Gloria afterward had been a success, that I had nothing to worry about, that I had made the perfect impression with everyone, and the positive comparisons with Shirley meant they already liked me. After his reassurance, I relaxed enough to fall asleep and woke up the next morning with my hand in his and a mark on my arm where it had rested all night across the center bar. I was to learn later from a relation in Shirley's more demonstrative family that this emotional distance and reliance on alcohol to grease the social skids, so to speak, was the Stoughton way.

On Monday morning, after a hearty breakfast and another comfortable and leisurely conversation with Gloria, we thanked her for the party and then set out for Hinsdale, New Hampshire, which was located at the point on the map where Vermont, New Hampshire, and Massachusetts come together, about a two-hour drive southeast of Fort Edward and Hudson Falls, which were already starting to become conflated in my

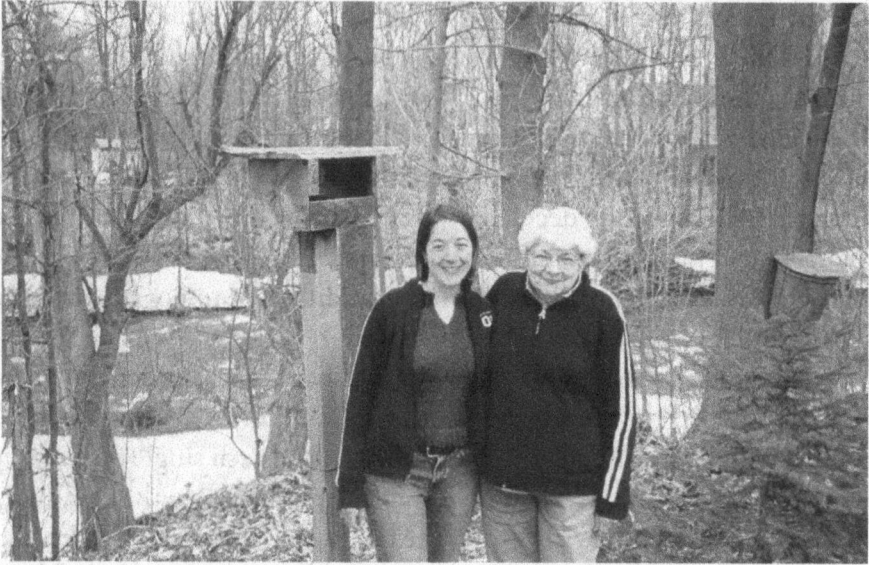

The two most important Stoughton women to me: Kensey and her grandmother, Gloria, taken at Skip's northern New York home the spring before I met them.

mind. This was my Thanksgiving break, and I had the whole week off from teaching, so we had decided to combine both family visits, spending time with his mom first and his daughter and her husband next. It would be another month before I'd have this much time off again. Some friends thought this might have been too much all at once, but we were in love and wanted to include those closest to us, and after the first meeting had gone so well, we headed southeast, full of confidence and anticipation. Most of our drive this day was through the idyllic Green Mountains of Vermont, and as we came down into the Connecticut River Valley at Brattleboro, Vermont, I could see that living in this region would have many of the same small-town charms as living in Fort Edward or Hudson Falls. East of downtown Brattleboro, where Kensey's husband, Tim, was a police officer, was the bridge to New Hampshire, where Kensey and Tim lived. Skip was already familiar with the area because he had helped them move here the previous summer, just before he met me. Shortly after crossing the river, we turned off the main road into an even more rural neighborhood where Kensey and Tim's raised ranch house was tucked below a hillside near the southern border of Pisgah State Park, which guaranteed that there would be no development on the land behind them and provided a built-in set of walking trails close to their home.

I knew that Kensey was a well-loved only child. Though Skip and Shirley had hoped for more children, an immune system disorder that led to a difficult pregnancy had prompted their doctor to suggest that, for Shirley's safety, another pregnancy would not be wise, so Skip had the snip. He had also told me that Kensey had donated a portion of her liver to her mother when Shirley needed a transplant, though the surgery had failed. After the previous relationship, which had taken him to northern New York, had ended, Kensey had been pressuring him to move nearer to them, so I was more nervous in some ways about this meeting than I had been about Gloria's party. Though it was a work day, Kensey had managed her schedule as a freelance music therapist so she could be home when we arrived, and she came bustling out to greet us before we could get our bags out of the car. Right away, I was charmed by this small, vivacious, dark-haired woman, her infectious energy, and her obvious affection for her dad. Based on the wedding picture of Skip and Shirley I had seen at Gloria's, Kensey was a mini-me of her mother. I hoped this delightful young woman would enjoy me as much as I was enjoying her right now. Skip seemed to relax soon after he introduced us, and I presumed he knew his daughter's signals well, so I was able to relax, too.

Knowing his love of gardening, and having been assured that I shared it, she gave us a quick tour of the yard, including the things she had planted since he'd last visited them the previous summer. Then she gave me a tour of the house while Skip tagged along, and father and daughter exchanged humorous barbs about the challenges they had experienced while getting some of the young couple's heavy wooden bedroom furniture and a couch up the central stairs to the main level of the house. "Good thing Tim and I are young and strong, old man," she teased with a hearty laugh, to which he joked, "That may be, but I'm still better at reassembling all the pieces than either of you," with matching good humor.

After the quick tour, we settled in to chat while we waited for Tim to get home from work. I had not yet morphed into the obsessive pho-to-documentarian I would become a few short years later, so my primary

Two couples enjoying each other's company.

memories of this first meeting with the most important people in my future are hazy and unfocused. But I remember that from the start I was comfortable with both Kensey and Tim in ways that I hadn't been with Skip's mom and his extended family, and I didn't require his regular assurances. I knew we were getting along well from the start. Our conversations were far-ranging and open, and I never worried that I was being grilled or judged. My inchoate worry that I might never measure up to her mother or be worthy of dating her father slowly vanished in the easy conversations we had over the next couple of days.

The second day of our visit, Kensey took us to the Yankee Candle mothership, about half an hour south, in Massachusetts. This was the first time I'd seen anything as fantastical as our local department store when I was a child, and the tenth floor had been over-the-top tricked out like a holiday fantasy every Christmas season. I was fascinated with both the candle paraphernalia and more Christmas ornaments than I'd ever seen in one place, but that charm lasted only about fifteen minutes, and then my introverted self, which hated crowds and was approaching serious overload, needed to be finished with shopping and crowds and on my way home again. I mentioned to Kensey that I was just about done-in with shopping, and without challenge or criticism, she asked me if I could manage a few more minutes while she showed me one more thing. At my nod, we left the guys and hurried away to see some spectacular blown-glass bird ornaments. I picked out one that reminded me of an ornament that had been on my childhood Christmas tree, and we rounded up the guys, headed for the checkout counter, and escaped retail excess.

After a long evening of engaging and far-reaching conversation, as we hunkered down in the guest room (in a queen bed with no bar in the center or separate linens), Skip confessed to me that the moment when we left the men in the dust and vanished into the crowd by ourselves was when he realized that everything was going to be fine. I acknowledged that Kensey's willingness to accept my need to leave without challenge made me feel understood and accepted. One other image I remember clearly from that first visit is while Kensey and I were working comfortably together, navigating the limitations of their tiny kitchen without words while preparing the turkey day meal, I looked up to see Skip watching us with a huge grin on his face. Perhaps he, too, had been more nervous about how this visit would unfold than I realized, but that Thanksgiving smile told me in no uncertain terms that he wasn't worried any longer.

The next day, we started for home around midday, hoping to avoid some of the end-of-holiday-weekend traffic and figuring most people would be shopping for those Black Friday deals so there wouldn't be many other folks on the road. On this last leg of our trip there was one more family member to meet. Kensey's Aunt Sue, her mom's older sister, had been like a second mother to Kensey for most of her life, a relationship that had intensified after Shirley died, and both Kensey and Skip wanted me to meet Sue and her husband, Bill. So, we had arranged to have dinner with them in their home in the southern Adirondacks and spend the night there before driving the last two and a half hours back to Canton the following morning. When we arrived at their home, Aunt Suesical, as Kensey called her ebullient relative, welcomed us with obvious affection for Skip and lots of openness and warmth for me. Bill

Kensey's beloved Aunt Sue and Uncle Bill, who became good friends to me, though there's no official word for our familial relationship.

was more reserved, taking a back seat to Sue's boundless enthusiasm, but also very pleasant, and both welcomed us without reservation. After only a few minutes, the reason for their enthusiasm became clear. Sue mentioned that she had just gotten off the phone with Kensey and was delighted to know that our visit there had gone so well. She didn't say it in so many words, but if Skip and Kensey both liked me, it seemed Sue was determined to like me as well. In fact, though there's no word in the genealogical lexicon for the relationship between a man's deceased wife's sister and his new romantic interest, Sue and I became very good friends as time passed and my relationship with the entire family deepened. This Thanksgiving adventure was just the beginning of my new life as a soon-to-be member of the Stoughton clan. Though it would take another several months before I met Skip's other brother, Mark, and his wife, Patty, who lived in western New York, they were also welcoming and became good friends over the years.

CHAPTER FIVE

COURTSHIP'S BUMPY RIDE

AS I PULLED into the hospital parking lot in Tualatin, Oregon, my heart started to slow. I'd been calm and cool for the last half hour with Mom and the paramedics, and even though I was about to find out what the damage was, she was in good hands. But first I needed some solace for myself. I pulled out my phone and dialed Skip in northern New York. It would be early evening there, and he picked up right away.

"Honey, I'm at the hospital with Mom. She fell in her favorite thrift store and had to be ambulanced here."

"What happened?"

"I'm not sure. I was looking at sweaters, and she was looking at jewelry, and I heard the weirdest noise, something between a grunt and a cry, and when I turned around, she was in a heap on the floor. I ran over and tried to help her up, but when she cried out loud at the attempt to stand, I knew it was bad. She's so damn stoic and never admits when she's hurt, but she couldn't fake her way through this one."

I was aware my voice was starting to shake, and my heart rate was going up again. I had to keep it together or I just might start crying. So, I slammed on my "I'm in control" hat and went on with my story. I knew I was getting sharp and brittle and speeding up as I detailed what happened, but it was the only way I could hold it together.

"She kept saying she'd be alright if she could just get home to take an aspirin and lie down. I could see that she was mortified by the attention;

she hates to be thought of as a bother to anyone. The manager called 911 as soon as he saw an elderly customer on the floor of his store, and when the EMTs came rushing over to her with the stretcher, I thought for a moment she was going to push them away, but then she calmed down and let them take care of her, so here we are."

"It's okay, sweetie, she's safe now. You can handle this; I know you can, but if you need me there, I'll be on the next plane."

"No, Mom would hate having you see her in the hospital for your first meeting. But I'll be calling often. Sorry for being so needy."

"No need to apologize, babe, hospitals are a bitch."

His calm demeanor and soothing voice in the face of my unsteadiness helped me get my fears under control, and his remark about hospitals was an understatement. I knew he had his own history with hospitals to contend with. His first wife had died in one after two failed liver transplants and a long, difficult stay. Most of the other men in my life had been attracted to my perceived strength and had left at my first show of neediness, and my former husband, though handsome and creative, had been so self-absorbed that he rarely paid attention to my needs beyond sex.

This was the first big emotional test of our new relationship, and Skip had passed! He was the first man, since my dad died, who listened to my needs without needing something from me in return, and he listened well and without judgment. Such a new experience for this independent woman. I liked it. I thanked him for helping me stay cool and told him I loved him, but I didn't hear him reply back to me as I broke the connection, so there I was in a sudden tailspin.

"That's never happened before. Was I too perfunctory and brittle? Or did my being at the hospital trigger a memory of Shirley? Why didn't he say it?"

I convinced myself I was overreacting and needed to hold onto the support and strength he had offered, so I took a couple of deep, centering breaths and went into the ER, where I found Mom resting in a small cubicle. The nurse said she had a hip fracture, but the doctor would have to look at the X-rays to know what to do next. My brother's name and phone number had been in Mom's wallet as the emergency contact person, and he would be on his way soon. Sitting with Mom while we waited for Toby and the doctor, I tried to get a handle on her mental state as well as her pain levels. A notorious stoic, she was refusing any serious pain medications at this point and downplaying the extent of her injury. She was pale but calm, though she was still fuming about why they hadn't just let her go home after the fall.

"You broke your hip," I countered, "And they tell me they might need to do some surgery to repair the damage."

"Phooey," she snorted, and all the bravado went out of her like a pin-pricked balloon. Mom already had one artificial hip from a fall she'd taken a decade earlier when she was just eighty. This time, she was nearing ninety and frustrated at having to go through it all over again on the other side of her body.

When Toby arrived, I noticed that his relationship with Mom's doctor was chummy. The feminist in me chalked that up to masculine preference, if not full-on gender bias; he was getting more information about Mom's situation in the first few minutes after arrival than I had been given in the hour-plus we'd been waiting for him. But when the doc left the room to go read the X-rays and decide what kind of surgery was warranted, Toby confided, "This guy is one of my clients; in fact, I handle retirement accounts for most of the docs at this hospital." My fury cleared. So thanks to my brother's professional relationship with the doctor in the financial realm, Mom got the best possible attention in the medical one, and we got more information than most families might get due to this sense of professional reciprocity. That same doctor later confided in Toby that he wished he had Mom's blood chemistry and overall state of good health, especially given the disparity between their ages. However, he still advised hip replacement surgery immediately, so they prepped Mom, and as they wheeled her into the operating room, Toby said he'd stay while I went back to the house for the evening. He hoped Debbie and I would be able to keep the boys from freaking out about Grandma Mary being in the hospital.

After dinner, we played dominoes with them until their bedtime, and then we drank wine together while we waited for Toby's return with the news that Mom's surgery had gone well. I got a sweet email from Skip later that evening, telling me how much he loved me, how sorry he was that I had to deal with this trouble, and how much he was looking forward to my return in a few days. Between that message, the relief about Mom's situation, and the wine, I stopped worrying about one missed "I love you" and slept very well that night. We arranged for Mom to go to a rehab facility for a few weeks when she got out of the hospital. Toby and Debbie had booked a vacation trip to Vietnam with her parents, something they'd been planning for over a year, and they feared they might have to cancel it, but I talked to colleagues at work who agreed to help cover my teaching schedule so I could come back in a few weeks to bring Mom home after rehab and initiate ongoing home healthcare services. My nephews were still young enough that they couldn't be left alone, but they didn't really need a full-time "babysitter" per se. Debbie had already arranged for a college-aged helper to live in for the duration of their travels, but I would take over some of her duties for the first few days while I got Mom situated in her own house and got her services started.

During Mom's first week back home, I was careful not to stay all day or overnight with her, using the excuse that I needed to be back with the boys when they got home from school. I didn't want her to get too dependent on me since I had to go home again soon, and we needed to see if she could be home alone without twenty-four-hour care before I left. She did seem a bit more spaced out than usual, but I explained that away because it was something that happened to lots of old folks after a major operation. And she was still taking some major post-surgical pain meds. I reassured her I would come back the following month for another short visit. She was disappointed that Skip would not be with me the next time. She had by now talked to him a few times on the phone and had fallen in love with his deep voice and pleasant manner. In fact, she was referring to him on occasion as her "new son-in-law" or "my daughter's husband," even though we had said nothing about getting married. In fact, Skip had explained to me when we first started getting serious that marriage would be out of the question for him because he was counting on survivor benefits from his deceased first wife's Social Security as a critical part of his retirement income. That hadn't bothered me, because I didn't have much faith in the institution of marriage, given my difficult first union. So it was convenient that Mom had us married in her head. It was clear that we were going to live together, and soon, so that would be an explanation we would never need to make to Mom since she'd done the imaginative work for us.

Even though marriage was not part of our plan, when I returned to northern New York after the holidays, Skip presented me with an interesting idea one evening as we were getting ready for bed. "Just because marriage isn't on the table for financial reasons, there's no reason we can't have a ceremony and a big party to tell everyone we are planning to share our lives," he reasoned. "It just wouldn't involve a license or a traditional wedding ceremony. We could even exchange rings. In fact, let me buy you a promise ring to seal the deal, and we can worry about the particulars later." Though his delivery had been more practical than romantic, and I had never been someone who yearned for a diamond, the sweet suggestion from this man made my heart dance. I liked the idea of making a public statement of our commitment, so I said yes immediately. We hoped to find a house to share soon, which would become the location for our combination housewarming and commitment ceremony. We joked about the mental health implications of the word "commitment," but that didn't detract from the seriousness of our plans. We decided that we would shop for the promise ring in Portland when we introduced Skip to Mom in person later that spring.

We both owned homes, so the first thing we did was talk about the pros and cons of each existing home. Skip had the more spacious house on a wonderful riverfront lot, but it would be a long commute for me and would mean I could not come home for lunch or between the regular workday and evening rehearsals, which my job required for at least one eight-week period each academic year. My house, though much more convenient to my work, was the smaller of the two homes and would require substantial renovation. It didn't take us long to realize that renovation would not be a cost-effective solution, and we were much better off looking for a different house for our new abode. In northern New York state, the winters are so fierce that most people take their real estate off the market during the cold weather, and there's always a surge of new listings in early spring. So, we started our house search slowly, knowing things would heat up as the weather did. But we were not idle in the meantime; other elements of our relationship continued to develop beyond the romantic. We completed all the required paperwork for registered domestic partners with my employer and enrolled Skip in the university's health plan right away. We also hired a lawyer and started the process of getting all the protections of marriage possible without the actual license—which turned out to be everything except Social Security survivor benefits.

In early April, Skip started experiencing some odd numbness in his right arm and shoulder but passed it off as a possible side effect of a new blood pressure medication he was taking. I was singing a solo in a choral concert at the university, so he came to our early evening dress rehearsal the day before the concert, after which we went to one of our favorite restaurants for a late dinner. We were seated on the glassed-in patio having a drink and looking over the familiar menu when I asked him what he was going to order. His response was total gibberish. At first, I thought I hadn't heard him right because of the noise level in that crowded and acoustically bright space. "What did you say?" I asked. The next time was no better, and I could see the panic rising in his eyes. He knew he wasn't making sense. I realized something was wrong. We got the owner's attention right away, and he called for medical assistance. By the time the ambulance was on its way, Skip's speech was back to normal. He was adamant that he didn't want the EMTs to come rushing into the restaurant, so we met them out front. By the time the ambulance pulled up a few minutes later, Skip was feeling normal again and didn't want any attention. I was reminded of Mom's stoicism about her hip only a few months before this, and I was having none of it. The restaurant owner had been through his own medical emergency and was able to talk Skip into letting the EMTs take him over to the hospital to get things checked out. So off they went in the ambulance, with me following in the car, heart pounding all the way.

At the hospital emergency room, there was a lot of waiting around until the technician was available to do a carotid ultrasound image. Once the test was underway, they quickly identified the blockage that had caused the problem. It would require surgery. They put Skip on blood thinners to prevent stroke, admitted him to the hospital for observation, and recommended that he be sent as quickly as possible to a major hospital three hours away in Vermont, because they lacked the ability to do the needed surgery in this small rural facility. It was after midnight, and the doctors told me to go home, get some sleep, and they would make the travel arrangements for first thing the next morning. After a more or less sleepless night, I returned to the hospital at seven the next morning, thinking I'd be picking him up for the drive, but Skip had already been dispatched by ambulance to Burlington, so once again, I followed in the car. I contacted Kensey and Tim. They would meet us at the hospital in Burlington, and by the time I found Skip in this new and much larger hospital, he was being prepped for a carotid endarterectomy, which the attendant jokingly called a roto-rootering of the carotid artery. The surgeon told us that Skip's arm numbness had undoubtedly been caused by the blockage, and he had seen evidence of a mild transient ischemic attack, or mini-stroke, but the mark was so tiny that he might have missed it on the scan if not for my report of the speech aphasia the night before. However inconvenient it seemed to Skip, who was feeling much better and would have preferred just to go home to rest, this event and the upcoming surgery would prevent a major stroke in the future, like the one that had felled his father when he was the same age Skip was now. I told him Kensey was on her way, and he agreed that "the boss lady" would insist that he have the surgery, so he stopped resisting.

The rest of our time in Burlington was a blur, but a few images stand out. Since we were not married, I had no legal right to any medical details, but Kensey let everyone think I was her mother by coming with me everywhere to get information and simply taking the lead when asking about her father. No one questioned my right to be there because she was so careful to include me in all conversations. She even let me be the first one to go in to see him in recovery after surgery, though I knew she was worried sick. The emergency—and sharing a hotel suite near the hospital—solidified the bonds that had begun the previous Thanksgiving.

When Skip was released from the hospital a couple days after his surgery, he looked disreputable. He hadn't washed or shaved for several days, and he had sunken eyes and a bandage around his neck with visible darker-than-normal red tissue showing around the edges of the gauze.

When the four of us went out to lunch in Burlington before heading our separate directions home, Kensey and I joked that he looked like he'd been garroted with a piano wire, and Tim ribbed him about what he might have done to deserve such treatment. He laughed, but I could tell how exhausted he was, and he slept most of the drive back to Canton. His recovery was normal, but he didn't lose that disreputable look for several more weeks, when he was able to shave again, and the scar from the artfully placed incision started to disappear into the folds of his neck. This made it easy to forget there had been any medical emergency at all.

By the end of April, I made another quick trip to Oregon to help move Mom into her new assisted living facility, and when I returned, Skip and I had an appointment to see a new listing for a house around the corner from where I was living. It was next door to one of my closest friends. The house had features we had been looking for, we loved everything about it, and we made an offer, which was accepted immediately. The closing date was set for the end of June. We were now ready to take that trip to Oregon to introduce Skip to my family and to see how Mom was settling into her new place.

Traveling together as a couple, like dating, is much different in your fifties than in your twenties, especially after the first exhilaration of romance has calmed down and routines have started to become more predictable. When I had traveled with romantic partners in my youth, I was eager to please and agreed to just about anything my current flame desired, putting aside my own habits or discomforts. Not so when I grew older. Older bodies, even healthy ones, don't tolerate pretenses, and facts, not fantasy, are the order of the day. Even at home, our days involved some variation of the following:

"Did you remember your pills this morning?"

"I'm too tired for that; let's rest before we go out again."

"My back is killing me; let's take a cab."

Our first plane trip together was quite an adventure for both of us and resulted in several revelations. It turned out that Skip loved planes but hated airports. Something about being in an airport made him nervous and edgy, perhaps because he had rarely flown in the past twenty years and wasn't used to the level of security involved in post-9/11 traveling. Because he seemed ill-at-ease to some random TSA employee, he was pulled aside for an extra search and questioning while going through security. When this happened, his face flushed, and he began to sweat, which made them doubly suspicious. I was able to come to his rescue by explaining the reason for our trip, even as the security folks got more challenging. My calm tone helped Skip manage the stress better and cooled the TSA jets a bit. I'm his direct opposite in that regard: airports are easy to manage for me—I've even joked through a random full-body search before—but I need drugs to fly without anxiety during takeoff and landing. Once we were seated on the plane, he held my hand and talked in his most soothing voice about how much he was looking forward to meeting my family, which helped keep me calm as the plane took off. So we navigated our travel complexities well together; a balanced pair.

When we arrived in Oregon, we went straight to my friends' house in northeast Portland, where we would be staying in their guest apartment while we were in town. Mom, who lived on the southwest side of the metro area, wasn't expecting us at her place until the morning of the next day, so we could relax for our first evening in the Rose City. Mary is one of my oldest friends, and I served as the "stage manager" for her wedding to her husband, Ted. Their marriage was now going into its third decade, and I considered them among my closest friends even though we lived on opposite sides of the country. I wanted them, almost more than anyone else, to like Skip.

When we rang the doorbell, Mary, a small salt-and-pepper whirl-wind of cheerful energy, came bustling out to greet us. Ted was upstairs on the phone, so Mary settled us on the deck in the spring sun. Her uneven rolling gait from a bout of childhood polio has never slowed her down, and in no time, we had glasses of a good Italian red wine and some nuts and olives to enjoy while we waited for Ted to join us. A gregarious and generous friend, Mary was predisposed to love anyone I loved, and she took to Skip immediately. He seemed equally comfortable with her, which pleased me greatly. By the time Ted appeared, Skip had become quite comfortable. Mary was a whirling dervish of social niceties, and Ted was a reticent but congenial mountain of a man with a thinning gray ponytail and an obvious pride in his loquacious wife.

When the sun disappeared, we headed indoors, where Ted suggested we take our luggage to the downstairs apartment. Skip led the way, but when he got to the bottom stair and turned to ask which way the room was, he suddenly disappeared, falling backward into the shadows. My heart lurched. Those big size thirteens of his had missed the narrow bottom step, and we found him sitting, a bit dazed, on the floor in front of the laundry room door. Luckily, all that was hurt was his pride, and Mary had to admit that Skip was not the first of their guests to take that tumble because of the poorly designed staircase landing, so we were all able to laugh and go on to the guest room. The evening was topped off with a delicious Italian dinner and conversation that felt as if we'd all been friends for years. I couldn't have been happier.

The next morning, we headed across town in our rental car to meet Mom and found her outside, deadheading the roses that lined the paths behind the facility. Skip and Mom already had a cozy phone relationship, so it felt like she was greeting a family member she hadn't seen for a while rather than an introduction. Once she showed us her little apartment, off we all went to see the house I had grown up in. It was an old farmhouse on an acre of land, different in style from Skip's childhood home but imbued with many similar memories. We gave Skip the tour around my family's small, eccentric home, full of antiques, books, and other curios, with faded

Mom and Skip enjoy visiting outdoors at her assisted-living facility before heading over to see our old house and get some lunch.

1950s wallpaper. It was the height of springtime in Oregon: plants were in riotous bloom, and Mom wanted to share that pleasure with us. Though she no longer needed the walker she'd been using after her surgery, she did need occasional help going up and down stairs, so Skip offered his arm, and she continued to hold on over the uneven ground as we took a slow stroll through the yard, where she told him about all the different flowers, shrubs, and fruit and nut trees that surrounded the house. I loved the fact that his enthusiasm for gardening matched hers.

After taking Mom out to lunch at her favorite local restaurant, we made the short drive to the next suburb to visit with my brother and his family. My brother's much newer house was palatial compared to the house we grew up in. Set up on a hill at the top of a cul-de-sac, with a manicured lawn and well-designed plantings all around, the house seemed to scream affluence and was emblematic of a quintessential suburban success story. But Skip didn't seem the least bit intimidated by these new surroundings and was as comfortable here as he had been in Mom's modest apartment and our old-fashioned family home. Though they didn't have the advantage of having talked to him before, my brother and his wife both took to Skip right away, and before long, the conversations were as relaxed as if they'd known him for years. Neither of them had liked my first husband. In fact, Toby had almost decked him once over some rude comment he made about the family, but everyone seemed to love Skip on sight, not least of whom were my nephews. The boys were both in middle school at the time and couldn't have been more different. Christopher, the older, was a sweet, dreamy, artistic soul, and Andrew, two years younger, was a more competitive, athletic, and outgoing personality. Skip seemed to know how to talk with each of them on their own terms, a skill I imagine he acquired in his years of teaching and working with high school students. It didn't take long for Andrew to figure out Skip had been a history teacher, so they found lots to talk about because history was Andrew's passion. And because he had been spending time paying close attention to my theatrical life in the months we'd been getting to know each other, Skip was able to show genuine interest in Christopher's recent performance in the school play. The afternoon and evening flew by. After dinner, Toby took Mom back to her apartment so Skip and I could continue visiting with Debbie and the boys, and any nervousness I had ever had about how my family would respond to this man I was learning to love more each day was put to rest,

Skip enjoyed getting to know my nephews while we were visiting Toby and Debbie.

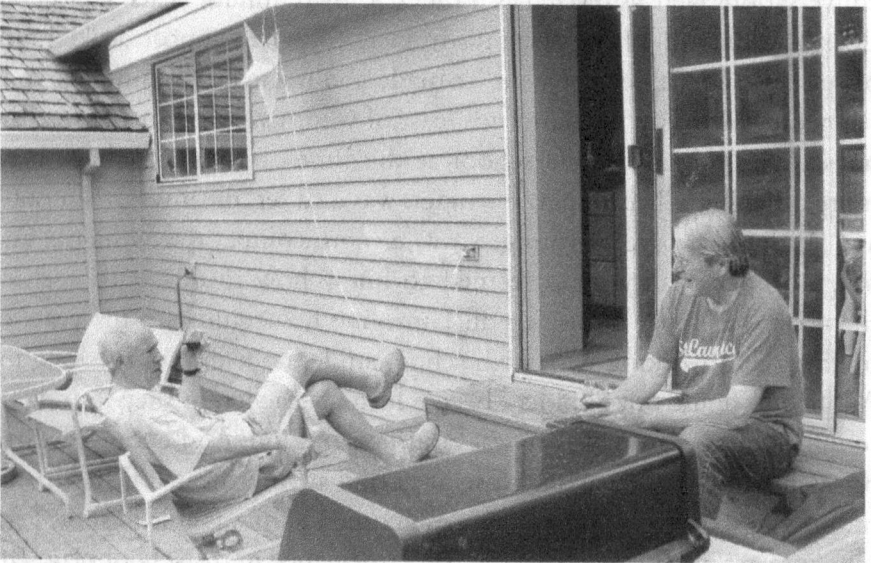

Toby and Skip get to know each other on the deck during one of our visits to Oregon.

and if Skip had ever been nervous about meeting my family, he didn't show it. We would visit with Mom each day, and with Toby and Debbie and the boys a few more times while we were in town, but the important work of introduction had been achieved, and now it was about having a good time visiting and getting to know each other better.

On our next to last day in Portland, Skip asked if it wasn't about time to go ring shopping. We went to the Hawthorne district in southeast Portland, an area known for its unique specialty stores. After walking up and down several blocks and in and out of many crowded stores filled with one-of-a-kind handmade items, I was beginning to despair of finding something that we liked that wasn't out of our price range. I was also starting to get that feeling of impending energy drain that came upon me when I got overstimulated by crowds in public places, which would mean I'd need to find someplace quiet and isolated to recover . . . and find it right away or suffer a meltdown. I told Skip that the store we were about to enter needed to be our last one for the day, and he agreed. Once inside, we told the salesperson what we were looking for—something unique and emblematic of our desire to make a life together but not a traditional engagement ring. She smiled and led us to a particular case, where she pointed out a delicate gold ring with a single milky-white cabochon moonstone set in the center, not unlike the size and shape of a traditional diamond solitaire but unique in appearance. She explained that moonstones were said to have calming and balanced feminine energy and association with love and lovers. I was quite taken with the look and the symbolism of this unique ring and tried not to worry too much about the possible price tag as she pulled it out of the case. It fit me well, and Skip liked the look of it, too. Were we both at the end of our shopping ropes, or was this a fortuitous find, or perhaps both? But we knew it was the ring we wanted. Best of all, the price was within our limit, so Skip pulled out his credit card and closed the deal. With our new purchase gracing my left ring finger, we headed for our car to return to Mary and Ted's for the quasi-engagement party they were throwing for us on our final night in town. Before we got in the car, Skip took my hand, looked again at the ring, leaned in to kiss me, and whispered, "We're now officially committed to be committed. I love you." And all of my fears vanished.

CHAPTER SIX

MAKING OUR NEW HOUSE A HOME

BEFORE WE COULD finish settling into our new house and focus on our ceremony planning, there was yet another trip I needed to make to Oregon in late July: to help Toby finish clearing out Mom's house. It had been sold to a developer who was planning to tear it down to build two contemporary McMansions. The property's value had appreciated exponentially since my folks bought the place fifty-five years ago, and the proceeds of the sale, placed in a trust, would pay the cost of Mom's care for many years to come. While we were relieved by the financial security the sale would provide, we were saddened that the house we grew up in would be bulldozed into the foundation hole. When I arrived, I discovered to my chagrin that Toby had given all the boxes I had packed for our new home on our previous trip to an antique dealer as part of a deal he had made a few days before.

"How could you forget that I wanted those things?" I demanded.

"Hey," he shot back, "when it comes to thinking about stuff, I'm just not that guy."

Toby and I could not have been more different in this regard. He was unsentimental, and I was the keeper of the family emotional lore, often triggered by objects that our parents had gathered and treasured during their decades in this house. In fact, as far as I could tell, my brother was allergic to emotionality altogether and hated being reminded of anything that smacked of feelings. It was why he wanted to be done with the house and everything in it as soon as possible. I let it go, though I was seething inside. Avoiding conflict or confrontation is one of my superpowers, so I used the energy of my anger and set about trying to get the items back.

To my amazement, within twenty-four hours, I was able to get back almost everything I wanted from the dealer, who was more embarrassed by the gaffe than my brother was. The boxes contained items that evoked fond memories from my childhood, including a Delft spice box with matchbox-sized drawers and ceramic handles with windmills on them. I remember that Mom used to keep whole sweet spices there, like cardamom, nutmeg, fennel, and cloves, probably more for their scent than for cooking. There was also a matching rolling pin and a bread box with the same blue windmill scene on the lid that had held Mom's homemade loaves for as long as I could remember. She had passed on her love for Blue Willow to me (her dining room had that pattern in the wallpaper), so I had packed up several serving dishes that I was more likely to display than use. Seeing that pattern, even on a serving bowl or a platter, made me feel nostalgic, and I hoped displaying them in the open space above our kitchen cabinets would give the new place an immediate feeling of home. There were also several vintage teapots and some delicate Belleek china items, including a sugar bowl and creamer, that Mom had ordered from Ireland. Neither she nor any member of her family had ever been to Ireland, though her mother had Irish grandparents. A couple of the items I'd packed didn't come back, including an antique fishing creel full of old lures that had belonged to my dad and a beautiful beer stein with an etched glass bottom that Skip had particularly admired when Mom had shown it to him. I suspect they were taken not by the dealer but by the young contractor working on the McMansion project after he heard Toby declare he didn't want any of the "stuff" Mom left in the house. Most importantly, though, all Mom's papers, letters, photographic slides, and scrapbooks were still safe in the chest of drawers where I had left them. These items, even more than the curios and keepsakes, were the repositories of the stories of our parents and their lives, and I wanted to create something with those stories, at least the letters and photos from the World War II years that Mom had saved so carefully for so long.

Once the mementos from my childhood were returned by the dealer, re-packed by me, and moved to my brother's basement, I enlisted my sister-in-law to be sure Toby wouldn't be tempted to sell or give anything away again. Because it was too costly to ship everything, I promised that Skip and I would drive back the following summer to haul all the items, including one large Victorian stained-glass window, from Oregon to northern New York. I remember when Mom and her best friend, Betty, had found those windows in one of their favorite antique stores. There were two matching rectangular panels salvaged from an old Victorian house; Betty took one for her home, and Mom had mounted her matching panel over the picture window in the living room. I had planned to hang mine across one of the large arched windows in our new sunroom, where I knew the beveled glass would create vibrant multicolored lights on sunny days in our new home.

Once I returned from dealing with Mom's house, Skip and I went to work on making our new house into the home we wanted together. After a hiccup in the real estate negotiations, our new house closed at the end of June. We were each able to find what appeared to be decent renters for our previous homes, and we were looking forward to starting our life together in a shared space that was new to both of us. However, we each had a furnished house full of memories and memorabilia, so one of our first challenges was to decide which items to bring to the new house and which to sell in a garage sale. Skip's furnishings were purchased when he first married nearly thirty years earlier. I wasn't sure how I felt about using all of Shirley's furniture, but the pieces had the advantage of being free, and I knew I wouldn't bring much in the way of furniture to the household because most of mine had been borrowed from what the theatre department called "the show barn," where we kept furniture that had been donated or purchased for use in plays throughout the years. When I had first started at St. Lawrence fourteen years before, arriving in northern New York just months after completing graduate school on the West Coast and without much furniture, our technical director had been happy to lend me several of the nicer antique pieces for my house, but I needed to return them. So despite some emotional discomfort at first, the physical comfort of his furniture won me over. The living room furniture would be from Skip's house.

His favorite items were the three recliners. Those chairs made me think of Goldilocks and the Three Bears because there was a Daddy chair (large and dark green), a Mama chair (medium-sized and rose pink . . . my mom would have loved this one), and a much older red one that wasn't a baby chair or even the "just right" one, but a comfortable extra that would be useful when we had guests. We had both been teachers, so we brought desks for our home offices. Mine was an antique writing desk from my grandmother's house, and Skip's was an old maple desk he might have shared with Shirley during their teaching careers. He had a couple of other antiques worth keeping: an old five-gallon stoneware pickle crock, a rustic Shaker writing box, a wooden trunk, a simple nineteenth-century wooden wardrobe, plus several nice maple occasional tables and a few other decorative items. Some of these had come from his years as the owner/manager of a small Adirondack hotel when Kensey was a child, including a number of bar mirrors (Stroh's, Captain Morgan's, Amstel, Molson) that had been given to him by sales reps in the late 1970s and were actually collectibles now in the twenty-first century. They found a perfect home on our new screened porch.

Skip had quite a collection of Shirley's framed color photographs, most of them flowers or landscapes, and they complemented my travel photographs of the Adirondacks, Ireland, and Nepal. I also had art (lithographs and watercolors) purchased through the years, and Skip and I eventually bought several paintings together. There were the inevitable lamps and side tables, and there I drew my first and only line. As I remember, it went something like this:

"Honey, we're going to use my Tiffany reproductions for accent lamps and ditch those boring lamps from your house. And we'll get rid of that weird Victorian table I inherited with the turbaned boy holding grapes. It gives me the creeps, and I'm tired of hiding that figured base behind the couch."

Turns out that unsettling table was actually a valuable antique that Skip sold to a dealer who also bought the wardrobe and the Shaker box. Skip had seen and approved of all my choices from Mom's house that were now stored in Toby's basement, and though we wouldn't have them in hand until the following summer, we would be adding Mom's teapots to Skip's mother's collection for display in our new kitchen, several

Our first living room together, showing a mix of our furniture and some of our artwork on the walls.

kitchen items in Blue Willow and Delft patterns that I was fond of would go above the cabinets, and more artwork, including a few of my grandmother's oil paintings, would add to the displays on the walls.

It was evident that we both had strong nesting impulses, trained by mothers who maintained eccentric households with touches of tradition here and there, so the trick would be how all that varied paraphernalia from our individual histories would work—or not—when we brought it all together. At this point in our relationship, we were both so happy to have found each other and eager to please, I doubt either one of us would have asserted enough dominance in the nesting process to cause conflict of any kind. But it turned out that we agreed on almost everything, neither one of us cared enough about any one item to fight over it, and we ended up liking the eclectic mix that resulted. It was a pleasure to discover that everything in our two households melded well into one, especially the many works of art we each had on our walls. In fact, once we had put everything up, it was hard to tell whose photographs were whose. It seemed that a chance social reference at Gloria's first party regarding Skip finding "another Shirley" was true in at least one particular: our photographic aesthetic.

Skip and I decided that there were only some minor refurbishing projects needed, and the biggest one was to repaint the sunroom, a large, casual space with a terrific view of the backyard. We both loathed the lurid lemonade yellow on the walls that the previous owner had been so proud of. At the paint store Skip surprised me by handing me a paint sample card with several rich shades of purple, one of my favorite colors, saying, "Sweetie, don't you think one of these would cover that awful yellow nicely?" I had expected him to go for a more neutral color based on the palette of his own house, and once I picked my chin up off the floor, I croaked, "Whatever you think, babe." For some reason beyond my ken, I have always hated house painting, and get frazzled by the activity, but he was not interested in hiring the job out to others, so he took the lead. As the shorter half of the painting duo, I spent most of my time near the floor molding and painting around doors and window sills while he spent more time on ladders and on the higher parts of the wall, and despite my initial trepidation, we got through it without a single argument or meltdown from me.

Because the three floor-to-ceiling, single-paned, arched windows in that room would have been too expensive to replace with more energy-efficient double-paned glass, and because there was already hardware in place for drapes, we invested instead in insulated drapes for all three of the huge windows, hanging the off-white drapes ourselves. We decided that replacing the old cabinet and drawer pulls in the kitchen with a more contemporary-looking design would spruce things up enough for us, and I used table runners and cloth napkins to disguise our decrepit old dining table, at least until we found a new one. This was the extent of our move-in refurbishments, and we were happy with them. Furniture, other than the living room set, was another matter.

One thing we didn't have between us for this larger place was a sideboard for the formal dining room. And we needed a new bed and several other small pieces. A few miles down the road from our town was an Amish settlement, so we headed out to Heuvelton to see what was available. Our first stop was at the Pickens General Store on the main street, where the furniture showroom, instead of being full of artfully staged displays, was packed with items crowded together so closely that it was hard to see the details of the work. But we knew the craftsmanship would be excellent, and with no high-pressure salesman in sight, Skip headed in to look around. I got sidetracked by the kitchen accessories in the main store until Skip came looking for me. "I think I've found our bed," he crowed, pulling me into the room full of multi-hued wooden furniture pieces in every corner. Who knew naturally finished wood had so much color! There was oak (both red and white), cherry, maple, hickory, and others. Near the center of the room was an unassembled Mission-style bed frame of red oak.

He pulled the headboard into an aisle. "See, simple but elegant. And sturdy. It's not too tall and ought to fit in that upstairs bedroom."

"Even with the slanted ceiling?" I wondered. So, we measured carefully and compared them to the dimensions we'd brought with us. Yes, it would fit.

He added, "There are two matching side tables and a beautiful chest of drawers we should get as well."

I'd never had such a fancy bedroom set, so I had no quarrels with his choice, only worrying aloud, "Can we afford all this?" I would later learn that my new life partner was an unrepentant skinflint when it came to most things, but when it came to furnishing our new home, he was no miser. But we still hadn't found the main item we came for.

There were no sideboards in this place, but the folks at the general store directed us to the Amish cheese shop at the other end of the street, saying that they had lots of furniture stored in the trailers behind the shop. In the cheese shop, we were directed to a large, unlocked trailer out back, and told that any item could be made in a variety of woods and sizes, so we should feel free to special order if we didn't find what we needed in the trailers; they would send word to Pennsylvania for what we wanted. As before, no salesperson accompanied us while we perused the contents of the trailer, which was even more tightly packed than things had been at the general store. And there was no electric light, so we browsed by opening the doors at both ends of the trailer and stumbling around in the dim interior. Eventually, I saw the perfect piece for our dining room but in the wrong color. After a bit more poking around in search of the same piece in a lighter wood, we had to admit that ordering a new piece was what we needed to do. I've never been sure whether we chose the lighter wood because of the lack of electric illumination that day or not, but it was a choice we never regretted, even though we had to wait a couple of weeks until it arrived and was delivered to our home by horse and wagon.

We had decided to fill the in-ground pool in our new backyard and reseed the area with grass rather than fight about whether the buyer or the seller would be responsible for the needed repair costs. On the day of the job, the excavator offered to discount his price, taking all the pool equipment in exchange for a significant reduction in the bill. Thrilled to be relieved of dealing with those items, we agreed. Our only worry was whether or not the new grass would come in before we were to host a large group of friends and family in the backyard in a little over two months; we were assured we should have grass by then.

We got our grass in plenty of time for the ceremony; not only that, we planted these two beautiful trees as well. Hard to imagine there was once a large in-ground swimming pool here.

We had set our ceremony for September 3. It would be the one-year anniversary of our first overnight date, and it had the advantage of being part of the three-day Labor Day weekend that year, so family members who needed to travel wouldn't have to rush home the morning after the party. The day after the ceremony would be Skip's mom's eightieth birthday, and because all of his siblings would be joining us, it would mean they could all celebrate Gloria's birthday together for the first time in many years. As soon as the pool was filled in, we began a daily habit of taking strolls around both the large backyard and smaller front garden to muse about what we wanted to do about gardens and landscaping for the ceremony and beyond. Flower beds and shrubs were my main passions; vegetables and planning a large raised bed for them were his; and we made shared decisions about new trees for the area that had previously been wide open because of the pool. We agreed that we wouldn't do anything dramatic before the ceremony, but we still took our strolls each day, dreaming about the future.

One morning, a few weeks before our event, we were meandering comfortably side by side across the new lawn, talking about possible fall plantings for the side beds, when I went down like a stone. I landed with one leg bent at an odd angle and the other buried in the ground up to the knee.

The suddenness of my drop and the startled expression on my face caused him to blurt out, "Honey, are you hurt?"

When I stopped laughing, I admitted, "The only thing hurt is my dignity, but I think I've lost my sandal underground, and the seat of my pants is starting to feel like I'm sitting in a swamp." He pulled me up, chortling, and I had to reach into the hole up to my shoulder to retrieve my sandal. I had hit a sinkhole where a corner of the pool used to be, and the dirt and some runoff from a recent thunderstorm had settled around an empty space just under the new grass that was holding the surface together over this muddy trap, at least until someone stepped on it.

"Thank goddess this didn't happen during the ceremony weekend," I quipped.

To which he replied, "Let's get a bag of topsoil to fill the hole. The grass should come back in time for the ceremony, and we can always put some kind of barrier around it if we need to."

We had about six weeks before the crowd would arrive, and I loved how calm he was about this substantial hole in our new lawn and how easily he could solve our dilemma. I was later to learn that this wasn't true for all situations, but when it came to gardening, he always knew how to fix things.

CHAPTER SEVEN

AUSPICIOUS BEGINNINGS

"THIS IS MY Beloved, and this is my Friend."

I heard Skip say those words almost as if in a dream. Even though we had together chosen this verse, from Song of Solomon 5:16, as part of our ring exchange, it didn't seem real to me until I felt the band with the Celtic knotwork slide onto my left hand. Maybe it was because my first marriage, held at the courthouse on a summer afternoon with only the witnesses required by law, had involved minimal ceremony at my then-husband-to-be's insistence, or perhaps because I still harbored some princess fantasies from my childhood, this seemed suddenly like the happy ending I had been waiting for my whole life. My heart was pounding, my throat and eyes were dry (which was weird because I felt like I might cry at any moment), and I wasn't sure at first that I could say my line loud enough for the friends and family spread out across our backyard to hear. But, veteran performer that I was, I took a deep breath, cleared my throat, picked up my prop from the sweet little attendant beside me, and turned to Skip, saying, "This is my Beloved, and this is my Friend," while sliding the matching ring on his large hand. Though the ceremony had no legal force, it had emotional power. And for me, this was much more of a true marriage, even without the license, than my first one had ever been. It was a good thing I only had to say those few words at that moment, because my throat closed up with emotion as soon as the rings had been exchanged.

We had decided to have a place near the end of the ceremony where guests could speak, if so inclined, and there were plenty who were eager to participate. In a group that included a high percentage of folks with either teaching or performance experience, or both, there were many comments wishing us well or otherwise adding to the festivities. Highlights included a Jewish friend, Steve, who told a story of why a glass is often broken at Jewish weddings. Though I have since discovered there's a lot of history behind that practice, our friend didn't talk about the sober elements of the tradition, instead emphasizing that the glass is shattered in hopes the marriage will last for as long as it might take to put the shards of the glass back together. Randy—a friend, member of the Lumbee tribe in North Carolina, and colleague in my department who taught a very popular course in Native American Oral Traditions— recited as his wish for us a Navajo Blessing Way prayer, the essence of which was, "May you walk in beauty and with beauty all around you." Skip and I had already selected the final blessings for the ceremony, and one was also Native American, so to close, Ron recited an Apache blessing that ended with the thought: "And if each of you takes responsibility for the quality of your life together, it will be marked by abundance and delight." Then Diane finished with a short Irish blessing, which she spoke in both English and Irish: "May you always have / Walls for the winds / A roof for the rain / And drinks beside the fire / Laughter to cheer you / Those you love near you / And all your heart might desire." The ceremony ended with everyone singing along to "When I'm Sixty-Four," and while we sang, I had a moment of laughing relief as I realized we had come to the end and no one had fallen through the lawn. After Ron pronounced us "committed" and decreed, "You may kiss . . . each other," the partying began.

When I returned from my trip to Oregon earlier that summer, all that remained of our ceremony planning had been to send out the invitations, plan the details of the event itself, and make sure the house and yard looked good for our guests. As far as the ceremony was concerned, we knew we wanted vows and an exchange of rings, for which I had brought back two beautiful matching gold rings with Celtic knotwork patterning from a trip to Ireland with a group of girlfriends earlier that spring. Without a marrying official like a judge or minister to preside over the ceremony, we had to decide who should emcee the event for us. One obvious choice was my teaching partner, Ron, known in jest as my work husband, who was also Skip's baseball buddy and fellow Red Sox fan. Though we were a terrific teaching team, Ron was much more than a colleague, more like a brother to me than anything: engaged and interested in my ideas, generous with his time and energy, emotionally available, and interested in my new life partner as a friend. The other obvious choice was our next-door neighbor and close friend, Diane, who often came over to hang out with us for drinks on the deck after her workday was over. Ron was a dynamic classroom lecturer, and Diane had been trained as an actor before becoming a lawyer, so we had no doubt they could handle the job. Folks told us later they thought we were either brave or crazy to turn them loose after giving them an outline of readings, music, and the vows, but we trusted them to be both entertaining and sensitive to the occasion in whatever they might have to say between the other elements of the ceremony. And they did not disappoint us. Skip's daughter, Kensey, had a beautiful soprano voice, so she could provide the music for the ceremony. She was a professional music therapist and an accomplished singer and guitar player, so we asked her to send us her ideas for possible songs from her repertoire that might be suitable for the occasion. She offered us several options on a sample CD; we accepted them all, especially "When I'm Sixty-Four" by the Beatles for the finale (we were both in our mid-fifties at the time). For our ring exchange, there were two sweet young girls near and dear to us who we asked to be our ring bearers, both of whom were about five or six years old at the time and thrilled to be asked to be in a wedding—any wedding—even a rather nontraditional one like this.

Once we announced what we were doing and when, we discovered that we had two other willing volunteers who expressed interest in doing a reading for the ceremony. One of those readers was Richard, one of my closest college friends and a regular theatrical collaborator, who would be coming up from North Carolina. He had known all of my college boyfriends and my first husband, as well as the live-in boyfriend who followed my divorce. He was well aware that I'd lived alone for the past fifteen years, and was thrilled to know I'd found happiness late in life, so he had decided this was an event worth traveling for. The other reader was Skip's brother's wife, Patty, though because this wasn't a legal wedding, I couldn't call her my sister-in-law-to-be. Food was informal, so we ordered several deli platters from the local grocery store, and a few friends volunteered to bring potluck appetizers. In the spirit of informality, we put several disposable cameras around the house and yard with signs that encouraged guests to take photos whenever they felt like it.

When Mom received her invitation, she asked Toby to bring her, but he refused, telling me on the phone, "That'll never happen," with no sense of how hurtful it was to me. I had sung in his big church wedding years before, but he didn't seem to invest in this event with the same kind of seriousness as his own. He knew and liked Skip and realized we were going to live together with or without any ceremony. I suspect his primary concern at the time was his worry that Mom shouldn't travel because of her recent hip replacement, increasing dementia, and a difficult adjustment to her new assisted-living situation, so I didn't confront him about it. It wasn't a fight worth having because so many of the other details were falling into place, but it would have meant a lot to me to have Mom there with us, along with Toby and Debbie. Skip's mom and all three of his siblings and their spouses were coming, as were Skip's nephew and his wife, because TJ knew his cousin Kensey would be there. They had grown up together and were the same age, the oldest of the clan cousins. Granted, all the Stoughton relatives lived in the state of New York, either in the southern Adirondacks or the Finger Lakes, so it was an easy drive for them. And of course, Kensey and Tim would drive up from New Hampshire. All told, there would be about seventy-five guests in our newly seeded backyard, and because we hadn't had any time to put our own gardening stamp on the new yard, we decided to get a few dozen white chrysanthemum plants to display on étagères framing the central ceremony location, which was over where the swimming pool used to be. We planned to give the flowers away to guests as party favors when the revelries were over. Other than the disappointment about not seeing my side of the family, our planning had gone well, for which I was thankful. I had sung in a friend's wedding years earlier in which a spat between the bride and her mother before the ceremony had nearly derailed the event, so I was beyond relieved that nothing like that had happened to us. Given the eventful early spring we'd had, we could have been more suspicious about what might yet be in store for us, but we saw this success as a reward for surviving the previous challenges, not a portent of things to come.

The afternoon before the ceremony, Richard's flight arrived in Ogdensburg, a tiny municipal airport about twenty miles away. We were also expecting Kensey and Tim to arrive in time to join us for dinner. Instead, we got a phone call that sucker-punched us both. Apparently, our few months of comfortable life with no surprises had been too much for Fate to allow. Instead of the "we're hitting the road now" call we were expecting, the sharp shift in Skip's voice alerted me that I needed to get on the extension and quickly. Kensey was being hospitalized for a tubal pregnancy that would have to be terminated right away for her safety. They had planned the news of her first pregnancy to be their wedding gift to us, and this Friday afternoon appointment on their way out of town had been a routine prenatal check until the problem was discovered. Kensey told us she had tried to persuade the doctor to let her come to sing for the ceremony and to do the surgery the day after she returned home. His answer was, "If you don't have this surgery right away, all those folks won't be celebrating a wedding; they'll be attending your funeral."

Kensey's tone was upbeat, trying to keep us from freaking out, and she implied that the doctor was overreacting, but it didn't work. This was Skip's little girl, so he was beside himself with worry, though he tried to match his daughter's upbeat tone while she was on the line. Once we hung up, this normally calm and imperturbable man couldn't stop pacing around the kitchen, breathing heavily. I had never seen him like this before, and I was glad Richard was there to keep him from going into a tailspin. He persuaded Skip to hope for the best for his daughter's surgery and to proceed as if everything else was more or less normal. After all, we were expecting seventy-five people the following afternoon, and Kensey had insisted there was no reason for us to cancel. In an unexpected role reversal, Richard poured the drinks while Skip sat, and as the men talked, I turned to the internet for more information about tubal (ectopic) pregnancy, which is how I deal with things I don't understand. Having never had a child of my own, I knew nothing of the risks and was soon to discover that ectopic pregnancy was rare and very dangerous. But now that Kensey was safely under medical care, the procedure itself was quite routine.

Once we both calmed down, we realized we had a few practical problems to solve before the ceremony the following afternoon. The first was easy: Kensey had sent us a disk with her music choices on it, so all we had to do was to set up an outside stereo system to play it, and Richard was more than willing to be our DJ. Next, my colleague and good friend Ann Marie agreed to help with the food prep, organizing the kitchen, and handling everything there. The last was more complicated. We didn't want certain family members, especially Skip's mom, who had experienced several complicated pregnancies and miscarriages of her own, to know the specifics of Kensey's situation until we knew that she had come through the surgery safely. A handful of key players would need to know what was happening, but we would do our best to keep the information from everyone else. We talked to Ron and Diane and decided that we would say Kensey's absence was due to an unexpected but minor medical procedure until we knew the results of the surgery, which was scheduled for first thing the following morning. We should have the news by the time the ceremony was over, and we could then tell Gloria the real reason why Kensey couldn't come. The deception worked since Gloria was heard to wonder aloud how Kensey had managed to get the CD to us so quickly amid her minor medical emergency.

The day of the ceremony was a hot, muggy one, and we set up tables on the deck with festive paper tablecloths. We also set up a small table near the entrance to the backyard with a guest book and programs for the ceremony, handed out by our charming young ring bearers. I'm a theatre person and this was a theatrical event, so we had to have a program, which included the order of events, the cast of characters, the technical support staff, and a special acknowledgments section on one side and humorous bios of the key players and lyrics for the closing song on the other. After all, how many people will know more than the chorus of "When I'm Sixty-Four"?

About an hour before the guests were to start arriving, Richard and I headed for the local grocery store to pick up our special orders while Skip set up the bar area. When we came out of the store, we discovered that there had been a brief but intense rain squall while we were inside. When we got home, we saw that all the paper goods we had set out before leaving were ruined, but after Kensey's news, what else could we do when Mother Nature piled on yet another inconvenience—one that might have challenged a different couple not yet seasoned through adversity—but shrug and keep going? The guests were due in less than an hour, and though the sky still looked threatening, we were determined to hold the ceremony outside. The reality was that there was no space in which to imagine the possibility of a rain location, though we did joke about emptying the two-car garage and trying to stuff everyone in there. We moved the food operation from the deck into the dining room, though the drinks bar stayed outside; we figured folks might brave a thunderstorm for a drink refill, and a drenching wouldn't hurt the bottled beverages. As it turned out, there was no more rain that day.

Though my relationship with Kensey was new, it was a good one, and I had really been looking forward to having her there to help me get ready for the ceremony, especially the elements that I thought of as "the girly stuff," like makeup, hair, choosing the right jewelry, and the like. I had a beautiful deep purple sundress with a layered, multicolored flowing underskirt, that I had asked our costumer to make for me for the occasion, and Skip had given me a unique necklace of silver-gray natural pearls on clear strands that made the pearls look like they were floating around my neck. I thought it was a perfect choice to go with the dress. He was going to wear khakis and a light blue raw silk collarless shirt he'd ordered online. It made him look quite dashing. I didn't realize how much I was looking forward to having Kensey tell me I looked good for the ceremony until she wasn't there to do it, but I soldiered through. After all, in my days as an actress, I had dressed myself for plenty of roles onstage; how different could it be to dress for one's own commitment ceremony? It was just another costume, right? In the end, I didn't have time to put on any makeup because I was too busy with other last-minute setup details, and my hair was a bit unkempt from all the running around, but Skip didn't seem to mind my natural look.

Once the guests were assembled in the backyard, Ron made a "pre-show" announcement about why Kensey and Tim were not there, and then the ceremony began. Sociologist that he was, Ron began by describing how this ceremony was different from a regular wedding ("the state has no part here"). He called attention to the fact that today's "production" had been written and directed by me, after which he launched into a humorous social history of oddball courting rituals and obscure marriage practices that had the audience chuckling. They included bringing a gift of a whale's tooth to the bride's family in Fiji, the happy couple in China killing a chicken and hoping it had a healthy liver, and a camel dance in Niger that did not require humans to dance as if they were camels but instead involved the beasts themselves.

Diane followed with what she titled "The Story of Skip and Rebecca," a saga she insisted would have been better told with sock puppets, though cooler heads had persuaded her to leave the puppets at home.

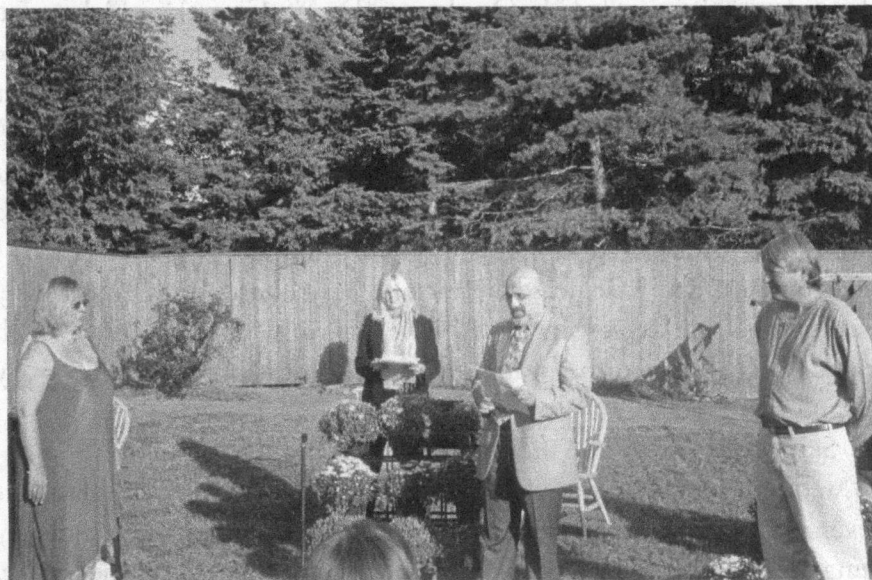

Ron entertains our ceremony audience with unusual marriage stories from other cultures; Diane waits to share her story about how we met.

Diane was legendary among friends and family for suggesting sock puppets would be needed to tell the most meaningful stories. Instead of
the epic puppet performance she had envisioned, she explained how
she and I had conjured Skip with a tongue-in-cheek boyfriend spell in
our women's ritual group. One of the key spell ingredients had been
"the semen of a righteous man," though we had to forego using that
element because we weren't sure we knew any to ask for a contribution.
When she began reciting the list of requests I had made for an ideal
boyfriend, including being kind, intelligent, and attractive, I couldn't
help but blurt out in unison with her when she got to the pièce de
résistance—"No comb-overs!"—which brought a hearty laugh from the
audience because of Skip's thick shock of silver hair. Diane detailed how
we met on the internet, with Skip finding me at work despite neither of
us paying our Match.com dues ("some might call it stalking"), as well as
the infamous "breakdown date."

Patty read a selection we had chosen from the I Ching. It began,
"When two people are at one in their inmost hearts, they shatter even
the strength of iron or bronze." Richard read a poem that a college friend
of ours had written called "In Our Image (Do We Create)," which ended
with the phrase, ". . . though we be two, we are one, / demonstrably the
fact / of the highest power divine. / And all of this, / this image and this
Spirit / and this power, / does not sum up the sum / of how I love you."
We had chosen a poem by Dorothy Colgan called "I Promise" as our
commitment vows, alternating stanzas until we spoke the last phrase
together: "I promise to love you in good times and in bad, with all I
have to give and all I feel inside in the only way I know how. Completely
and forever." The ceremony ended with the ring exchange, after which
friends had a chance to speak, and the closing song. Then the party
began.

Skip lived up to his nickname by bartending for his own pseu-
do-wedding, and there was plenty of finger food to go with the abundant
beverages. Skip's mom made a plate of shrimp for Sophie, our endlessly
hungry cat with a thyroid problem, in hopes of luring her off the serving
platters on the dining table, which only encouraged her to look for more,

Our "official" commitment photo.

though after a few drinks, no one seemed to begrudge her the shrimp. Skip provided good cigars for anyone who wanted to enjoy a celebratory smoke on the deck with him later in the evening. Only a few of the guys took him up on that, and none of the women, but there's a fun photo someone took with one of the disposable cameras that shows all the Stoughton men together with their stogies.

The party was long and festive, though I remember that after a few drinks, Skip's younger sister, Nancy, now a mother with adult children, admitted that she was still mad at him for being such a tough teacher in high school. Being seven years older than his next closest sibling, Skip had ended up being the history teacher for each of his siblings as they went through Fort Edward High School. Sometime early in the post-ceremony celebration, we got the good news that Kensey's surgery had been successful and she was now comfortable and resting, and she would be going home the next morning, so Gloria could finally be told the truth about what had really happened to keep Kensey from being part of the ceremony as well as missing Gloria's birthday celebration the following

Gloria celebrates her eightieth birthday with all her children on the morning after our ceremony.

day. The child that was lost in that procedure would have been Gloria's first great-grandchild.

Between the good news, the good day, the good food, and lots of good booze, we went to bed feeling blissful that evening, cuddling tight as usual. I don't think anything, even a more traditional wedding, could have made us happier.

CHAPTER EIGHT

DISCOVERING OUR NEW LIFE TOGETHER

AFTER OUR TUMULTUOUS early courtship filled with medical challenges, culminating in the commitment ceremony in our new home, we were pleased to find ourselves in a predictable—one might even call it boring—routine. In fact, the next few years seemed downright normal and more or less uneventful. However, I wasn't sure I knew how to do normal. After the initial euphoria had worn off, my first marriage had been fraught with emotional abuse, mostly gaslighting about my creative abilities from my musician ex-husband, who, while attracted to my singing talent as a prerequisite in a mate, didn't like to share the spotlight. It had taken me close to five years to figure out that he was one of the reasons I had regular migraines and needed a mouth guard at night. I was grinding my teeth so hard I had to use denture adhesive to hold it in. And it took another three years to realize that there was no rehabilitation possible, that he would never help me find a solution, refusing to go to counseling or even, near the end, to participate in creating the "no-fault" Oregon application for divorce, other than agreeing to sign if I took care of the paperwork. His insistence that he still loved me and could have stayed with me forever, and the accusation that it was all my fault our relationship wasn't thriving sent me to both pain therapy for the headaches and counseling on my own, where

I finally realized that it was his narcissism that was the root cause of my unhappiness. While this realization freed me to let go of that marriage, it also left me with an enduring wariness of intimacy, which in this first marriage had been conditional. The first year with Skip had provided enough distractions to keep me worrying about other, more immediate issues. Now that there were no medical emergencies, getting used to the fact that someone professed he loved me and didn't need me to prove myself to him was, frankly, scary and took some getting used to. I wanted things to work between us, but based on past experiences, I wasn't sure I could expect it to happen.

In the days following our ceremony, I went back to my teaching job at the local university, and Skip continued to enjoy his early retirement. Using the skills gained during his years as a hotelier, and much to my delight, he took over the general management of the household, including cooking and laundry. However, his cleaning skills left a bit to be desired, so eventually, he gave in to my insistence that we hire a cleaner to come in once a month for a deep cleaning, especially of the kitchen and the bathrooms, a practice I'd kept up for all my years of living alone before I met him. I was not one of those women who found satisfaction or relaxation in cleaning her house. In fact, it stressed me out. When details of our new roles and routines became known to friends, one of my colleagues in the department, a married gay man, gushed to me, "Honey, I'm jealous. I want a wife just like yours!" We also continued to travel, mostly to visit family, but now our travels were about the pleasure of visiting and not beset with unexpected medical complications and stresses for us or our family members. It had taken her some time to adjust, but my mom was starting to enjoy assisted living, and Skip's mom had, entirely of her own volition, sold her house to one of her grandchildren and moved into a retirement community with a direct link to nursing care, so we had no immediate worries about our mothers. We knew that despite their disappointment over their initial pregnancy challenges, Kensey and Tim were eager to start their family, so we had high hopes for grandchildren in the foreseeable future.

Because we had already bonded over gardening and decided who was to be in charge of which kinds of plants, the first major project we did

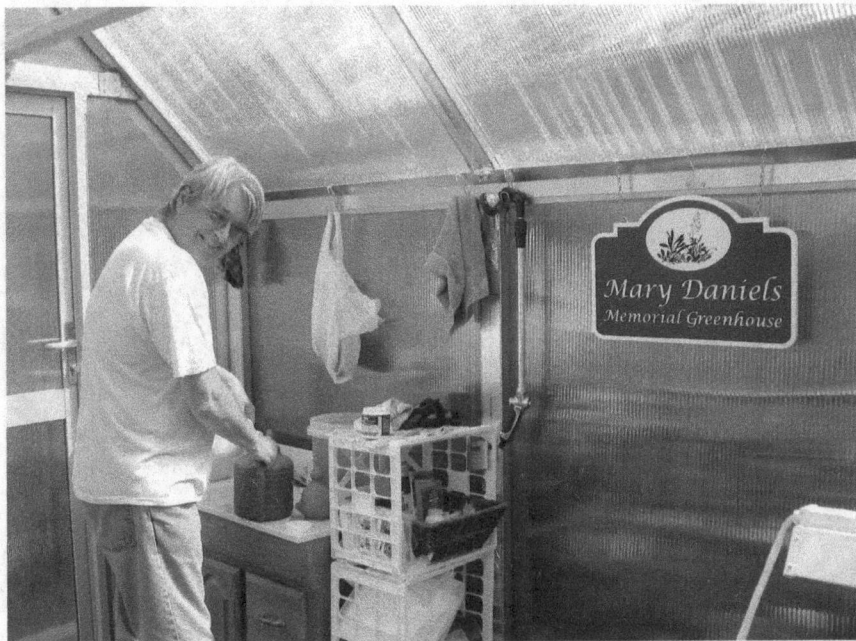

Skip mixing fertilizer in his greenhouse, and the new shrubs and spring flowers I planted near our deck.

*Skip's veggies, our herb garden, and
the new trees that became the yard's
centerpiece.*

together was to design and make a spring plan for our backyard (about a quarter of an acre surrounded by a high fence). Now that we had the pool filled in, we had a wonderful blank canvas to play with, and we envisioned all the garden and plant beds we wanted. When we moved in, the back deck had been old cedar planks that needed either serious refinishing or full replacement, so we hired a contractor friend to make us a new deck that would never need to be resealed or replaced, and I started to plan flower beds and paths nearby. There were already large peonies near the fence, and I added a forsythia shrub, baptisia, weigela, clematis, and lots and lots of perennial flowers for a riot of color at varying heights next to the deck. For his vegetables, Skip built an extensive length of raised beds along the north side of the back fence using railroad ties for the outer edges. He was a devotee of the square-foot gardening method, and he had worked out all the squares he needed in his 5-by-25-foot patch to accommodate the various veggies he wanted to grow: several varieties of tomatoes, both hot and sweet peppers, and lots of beans, for which he created a web of strings up the fence beside the raised bed. And herbs, all kinds of herbs. Eventually, we added some potatoes. We finished the backyard plan with two double-flowering crabapple trees on either side of where the diving board for the pool used to be. Over the years, the landscaping plan expanded year by year, and it always involved a special walk through every inch of the yard each spring to decide what we would add, subtract, or do differently in the coming summer months. That yard became a beautiful sanctuary for us and gave us great pleasure together, even if we weren't always working on the same parts of the property at the same time. I have never felt quite so much at peace as I did when I watched him work his veggie plots as I tended my flowers and shrubs, and I was looking forward to growing old with this man who loved working in the yard as much as I did. My trust in him started to grow with the gardens.

The end of each gardening day during the warmer months brought a new tradition for us on our deck: we surveyed our domain, enjoying drinks on the deck and validating our handiwork. At first, it was just the two of us enjoying the fruits of our labor and talking about the next steps in our design. But then it started to gain some traction with friends and neighbors who enjoyed coming over at the end of the work day to unwind and hang out, so "Drinks on the Deck" became a regular social event. It was during these times that Skip burnished his reputation as The Bartender. Everyone knew he'd run an Adirondack hotel in earlier years, but now he was the most desired host on the block: generous with his pours and ready to make any cocktail that was ordered, though it was clear he was a traditionalist and wasn't enamored of fizzy or frothy drinks. Relaxation was the order of the day during Drinks on the Deck, and not many days passed without some time outside, with or without our neighbors, enjoying the haven we had created together.

As the fall semester neared the winter break that year, I realized I was eligible for a research sabbatical combined with a long-postponed overload leave, which added up to three semesters off with pay, during which I was hoping to produce enough research to get promoted to my long-held goal of full professor on my return to teaching. However, having me take a half year off was a personnel hassle for my small department, so with his accountant's hat on, Skip ran the numbers to see if we could handle me taking a second full year off at half pay instead of a single semester at full pay. And with careful money management, we could do it. Our household roles wouldn't change, but we would get to see each other much more often in the spaces of my workday, and I didn't have to direct any plays with students while on leave, which meant our evenings would be our own for two whole years.

One of the other benefits to this situation was that instead of trying to figure out how to drive out to Oregon during the brief summer months, we could take a long cross-country driving trip early in the first autumn of that two-year non-teaching period (fall 2006–spring 2008), and that seven-week trip became both our honeymoon and a utilitarian necessity to retrieve the stored things from Mom's house that I wanted to keep. Our trip took us across southern Canada, down the West Coast (stopping for a week with family in Oregon), then, with our car full of those household goods and family memorabilia that we'd retrieved from my brother's basement, we headed into the desert Southwest for a few weeks of tourist sightseeing, followed by a long diagonal drive back to western New York for a visit with Stoughton relatives before heading home. It was on this trip that he earned the new nickname "geezer model" because he was a regular and willing photo subject as I documented our travels. Our ability to travel together, and his easygoing temperament as we made our way across the country with no disagreements or challenges we couldn't meet together, added more solid links to the chain of trust that was being forged between us.

However, once we were home again, Fate decided that after all, I was a theatre person, and we'd had enough time without drama. It was just a day after we returned home from our travels when it happened. In fact, we hadn't even finished doing the accumulated laundry from our last days on the road when I got a call from my mother's assisted-living facility. They couldn't locate my brother, who wasn't picking up his phone, and they told me that Mom was "unresponsive." They hadn't been able to wake her that morning and an ambulance was on the way to take her to the hospital. There wasn't much I could do at a distance, but I did finally locate my brother, who had been taking his morning run when they made the call to him. He said it sounded serious and suggested that we immediately get plane tickets back to see her before it was too late. He would head right over to the hospital and keep me posted. It was no more than an hour later when he called back to say Mom had died of a stroke without regaining consciousness, so now our trip west was to plan and execute her memorial and burial. She was just three weeks shy of her ninety-first birthday and had been struggling with moderate dementia but otherwise had seemed quite healthy for her age. I was glad we'd had a chance to spend time with her just weeks before this unexpected calamity and even more thankful that she died in her sleep before Alzheimer's could rob her of more of her personality and memories. I wrote and delivered her eulogy at a small graveside memorial with close friends and family. I remember the comforting feeling of Skip standing close behind me on that cool and cloudy late-October morning, supporting me both literally and figuratively as I completed this monumental task. Here was yet another reason to have confidence in this man. We returned home, exhausted from back-to-back travels, and hunkered down for a couple weeks of rest and recovery.

Then our normal life began again, this time with me trying to work on my sabbatical research projects. However, while I was in a take-charge-and-get-things-done mode immediately after Mom's death, I hadn't processed how deeply affected I was. When I tried to return to intellectual work, my brain wasn't working right. All I could think about was the loss and the memories. For many weeks. I went upstairs to my home office, hoping for a breakthrough but not having anything substantive to show by the end of the day. And those days kept getting shorter as I acknowledged my inability to concentrate on work and started coming downstairs in frustration earlier and earlier each day. Skip, ever eager to help, ran some more numbers for me regarding the long-term financial rewards of that desired promotion. Eventually he declared that because I was close to retirement, the money differential wouldn't be that dramatic if I didn't get promoted after all, giving me permission to give up that ambition, if I so desired. And it turned out that I did desire it. Very much.

Much of my professional life as an educator had been framed by the progress toward full professorship, but when it came right down to it, I wasn't as invested in that outcome as I had thought. It was a great relief to be able to say to myself, "This isn't as important to me as making time for my emotional life, something I've been putting on the back burner for years." Giving up that drive for promotion freed me, emotionally and intellectually, to pursue things that interested me the most without a care for their effect on my career near its end, and those projects laid the groundwork for the books I finished only after retirement from academic life. Further, this decision helped me to finally learn to start living in the moment, not worrying about what the necessary next steps would be. I could be present in my relationship with my life partner for the first time in my life. This was not always the most comfortable place to be, given my tendency to doubt myself or to worry about the future, though it was certainly the most authentic I'd ever been in my daily life and relationships. Ever.

The following spring (early June 2007), we became grandparents with the arrival of a lovely baby girl, to the delight of everyone in the family. As a childless woman, the concept of becoming a grandmother wasn't one I knew what to do with at first, but as soon as I held that child in my arms, I knew that love had little to do with bloodline and everything to do with choice and commitment. As an adopted child with a wonderful family experience, I should have known better, but I hadn't trusted it, not entirely, until I experienced it for myself. It was a blessing, pure and

Grinning Granny, and four generations of the Stoughton clan.

simple. And I had the good fortune to be part of an extended new family that didn't differentiate between step and real, not when it came to the grands. There's a photo of me with Maren as an infant that Skip instantly dubbed the Grinning Granny portrait, because it was evident that I was over the moon about this child. I know everyone says their grandkids are cute, but Maren was a true beauty, almost angelic; everyone who saw her said so. And her sweet nature was obvious to everyone who met her. We traveled to meet her the day after she was born and visited often during her early years. And like all grandparents worth their salt, we spoiled her, even brought her a fashionable baby dress from Paris, bought while traveling to Europe to visit friends and family just months after her birth. Experienced teachers that we were, we also started a college fund for her and gifted it to her folks for her first Christmas.

For another year or so, we continued to enjoy a pleasant, even placid, lifestyle with little excitement. I started to get used to the idea that life could be this calm, this balanced, this pleasant, without holding traps or future consequences. And I liked living this way. Our travels took us to visit close-by relatives, including Skip's mom and, of course, that new grandchild, but mostly we just returned to the comfortable and happy life we anticipated would be ours for years to come.

Our biggest excitement came when Skip reached the age when he could finally receive the survivor benefits from his first wife's Social Security, the ones that had kept us from legally marrying. He was bursting with energy when he returned from his visit to the local office, calling out as he came in, "Honey, we can get married after all!" Turns out that if you remarried before you started receiving benefits, they were lost to you forever, but if you remarried after you were on the benefits, they didn't disappear. So, we started to plan a "real" (as in legal) wedding, which turned out to be an abbreviated re-run of the original commitment ceremony—which Diane and Ron were more than willing to recreate—but for a much smaller audience, consisting only of Kensey and Tim, and Kensey's Aunt Sue and Uncle Bill, who had gone in our place to help Kensey with the aftermath of the pregnancy emergency. Of course, two-year-old Maren was thrilled to serve as our flower girl, and a local judge who was a friend of Diane's did the legal honors in our backyard. Now we were an official married couple, but all that changed were some legal issues around future inheritance. What didn't change were our feelings; we'd made a long-term commitment to each other, and this wedding was a minor event compared to our commitment ceremony almost three years before.

Shortly after the wedding, we encountered another medical emergency for Skip, the first one since his carotid endarterectomy three years previous. This time, the Big C came into the conversation, but the specialist who was to do the surgery told us that thyroid cancer was the best cancer to have. It didn't travel to other parts of the body, and it would be easily removed and controlled for the future years. The long-term prognosis was excellent. As a result, this new challenge didn't seem as frightening to either of us as that earlier surgery.

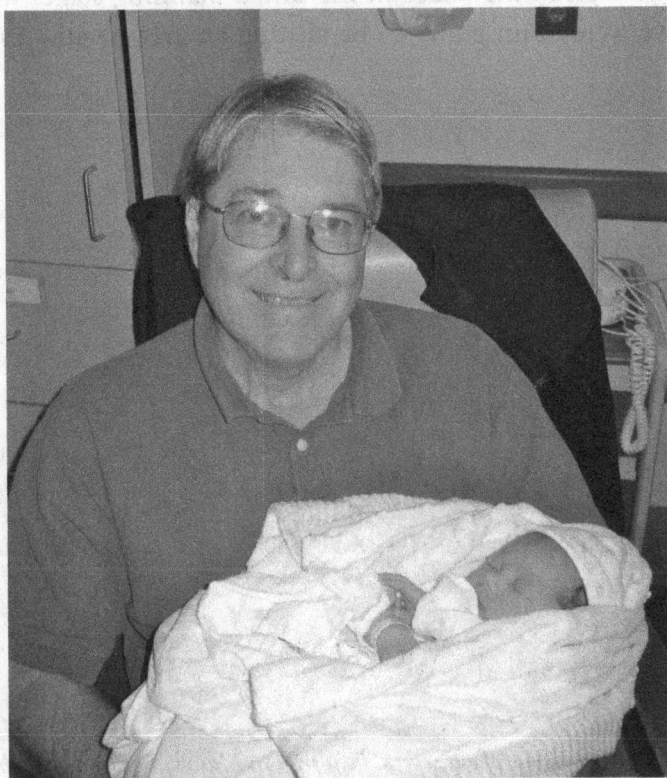

Papa meets Trenton for the first time.

Two years later, in May 2010, another grandchild came along, this one a feisty little boy as different from his sister as the proverbial chalk and cheese. He enthralled us all with his lively demeanor right out of the gate. We met Trenton the morning after his birth, having stayed at the house with Maren while her parents went off to the nearby hospital. The photos from that morning show Skip's delight at this new member of the family. The idyllic summer that followed brought us to a family wedding in the Adirondacks where Maren was, once again, a flower girl, and Trenton attended in a baby pack on his father's chest while Kensey served as matron of honor for her cousin's bucolic outdoor marriage ceremony. We also took a summer holiday trip for a few days with Oregon friends Mary and Ted, enjoying boat trips on the Maine coast (lobster boat, small sailing boat, and a large racing sloop, all within two days) and drinking wine and eating lobster and blueberries by the sea. This excursion had given me pause in the initial planning stages when Skip told me we were again going to be visiting an area he and Shirley had

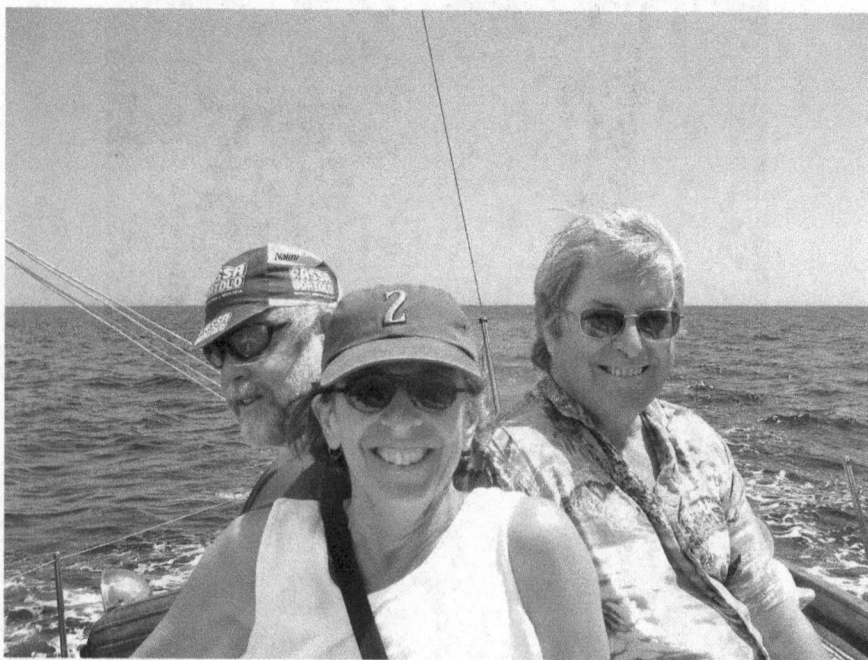

With Mary and Ted on one of our several boat trips in Maine just two months before Skip died.

come often, but during our time in Maine, there was never any hint that he was thinking about the past. He just wanted to share a place he loved with the woman he loved, and I learned to see the area through his eyes without worrying that he was thinking about someone else. I do believe another little piece of my armor released during that trip, and I relaxed even more into confidence in his unconditional tenderness for me.

In late August 2010, I returned to the start of yet another academic year, one that included directing the fall play at the university. Things were now going so smoothly for us on all fronts that we were sure we'd found a shared routine we could live with for many, many years to come. There was no way for us to anticipate that in just a few weeks, everything would be upended again, this time in a much more dramatic and permanent way.

PART TWO

꧁꧂

ALONG THE GRIEVING ROAD
(Grief Journals and Short Essays)

CHAPTER NINE

FINDING SOLACE IN WRITING

AS MUCH AS I love to write, I've never kept a regular journal, writing instead in fits and starts as my life experiences made it useful to document what's happening, and writing about it helped me to process my feelings. While I was a prodigious letter-writer back in the day, and often engage in extensive email correspondences now, I'd never envisioned "Dear Diary" as a person before. After three weeks of living in shock and moving through events in a fog of not knowing what was happening, and with a substantial measure of denial still affecting me, I decided to start writing about my daily experiences, addressing my thoughts directly to Skip. I missed my daily conversations and interactions with him, and decided to tell him everything I could remember about what it was like to learn to live without him. Was I hoping that by journaling, I could finally come to terms with his death? I know I found solace in the activity during the first weeks and months after his death.

I began on October 31 by confessing that I was feeling fragile and shared my obsession with wondering whether the day could have gone differently if I had been home:

> In spite of the fact that everyone tells me I shouldn't think about this, I can't stop wondering whether things might have been different if I hadn't been off to a meeting that Saturday and then grocery shopping right after. The ER doc said you had likely been

dead for a while when the EMT techs got there, which was only a few minutes after I came home and found you "unresponsive," and since everything looked peaceful, he believes that you slipped away into oblivion without really knowing what was happening. If you hadn't been sitting under that sunny window and felt so warm to the touch, I might have figured it out for myself. Or I might have been in denial, no matter what. I had been told by the doctor that even if I had been sitting next to you, I might not have noticed anything unusual, but I can't help wondering: did you know anything was wrong? Were you feeling normal that morning? You acted like it was a day like any other when I kissed you goodbye, but I know that you never liked to talk about it when you were feeling under the weather. Did you feel it coming, or did it catch you unawares, as it did me?

I invoked the prismatic light that had been bathing his body when I found him and acknowledged that I felt his presence in the regular appearance of those prisms in our house. I told him that decades ago I had felt my father's spirit pass through my chest on the night he died, and that I wanted to feel his spirit visiting me as well. According to pagan tradition, Halloween was supposed to be the night when the veil between the living and the dead was said to be the thinnest, so I was hoping for a visit from Skip. But it didn't happen.

While there was no longed-for spirit visitation on Halloween, I experienced a visceral jolt a few days later, on November 2, when I went to the dress rehearsal of the play I could no longer focus on directing. I made my way to a place where Skip and I had enjoyed watching regular productions over the years, and "I moved into the second seat without thinking, leaving the aisle seat open for you, with your long legs and big feet. Then it hit me that you were never going to be sitting there with me again, which made me gasp." The play revealed the dramatic loss of a loved one for one of the characters, and I admitted that the only way I could relate to the script now was through its sense of tragedy.

A couple of days later, on November 4, I wrote to Skip about my newest source of anxiety: that I would be cut off from the family I had come to love through what I referred to at the time as the familial equiv-alent of "last hired; first fired." This had been triggered by a reference by my stepdaughter to me still being young, someone who would find someone else soon, which I worried was a hint that she wanted me to leave now that her dad was no longer there to connect us. Not only did I write my detailed fears to Skip, I wrote his imagined responses as well.

"I know you would counsel me to simply wait to see what happens and to trust things will turn out okay, but I'm feeling so isolated and bereft that I'm not sure I can do that," admitting a few hours later that his suggestion had been correct, and I was feeling better and more in control of my fears after exploring them with my words.

Two days later, on November 6, I returned to the idea that if I'd been home, Skip's sudden cardiac arrest would have come out differently, admitting that the idea keeps bothering me "like a scab I can't keep from picking," but this time I started rationalizing:

> I know in my head that even if we had been able to bring you back from the brink of death, it's likely you wouldn't have been yourself any longer, which I know you would have hated. Kensey and I have talked about this, but my heart's having a hard time letting go of the possibility of being there to save you to continue living as exactly the same man I love so much. However, the reality is that the same "fate" we used to talk about bringing us together has also torn us apart.

That same night was the eve of what should have been Skip's six-ty-third birthday, and someone had given me something new to fixate on, which I tried to work out with my missive to Skip:

> A friend said something to me today about expecting that you would be waiting for me "on the other side," but that comfort is hard to hear when I know you already have another wife on the other side. I know this is how some people learn to live with the loss of their loves—this sense that they will be reunited again in some distant, spiritual future—but that's not going to work

for me. I know you still loved Shirley, even though you said you got over missing her once we got together. I also know that you loved me very much, but you had over 25 years with her and only six with me, so what does that mean "on the other side"? If you've been reunited with her, where does that leave me? Do I go alone into the afterlife, or will I meet you both there? I'd always thought I would have liked her if we'd met in this life, but will we all be in a place where the love will be shared, with no jealousy or possessiveness, or is it an immense darkness (or light, perhaps) in which we exist as ethereal beings with no need at all for human connection?

I see you every day . . . in the "geezer model" photos around the house that I love so much. In these images, I remember our joy. You were such a great travel companion and photo subject— always willing, never crabby about it, and oh, so handsome! We were happy together, working in the yard or sitting on the deck, enjoying a drink and a view of the haven we had created together.

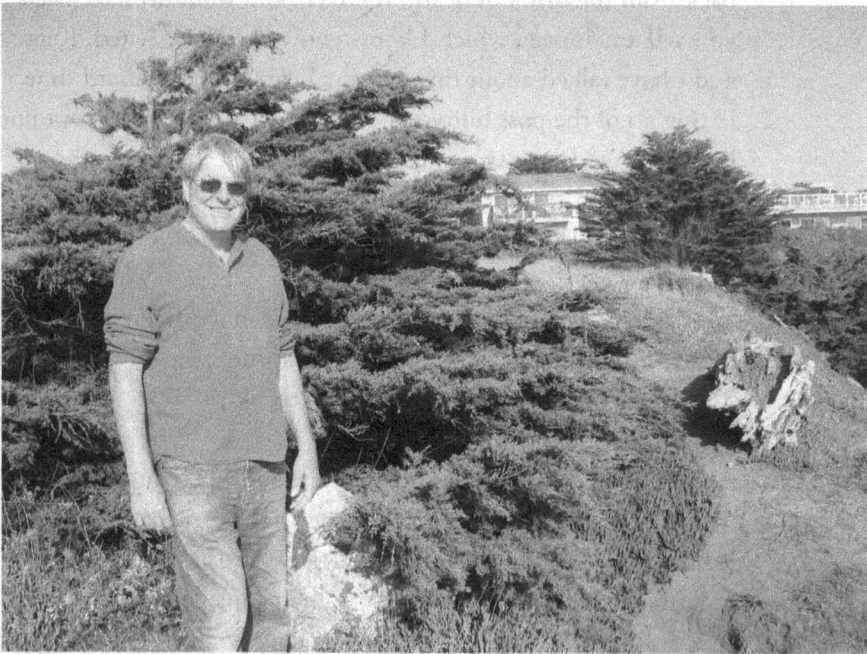

One of my favorite geezer model photos, from a trip to Mendocino County, California.

I remember that not every moment was joyful, but all things considered, we had a wonderful and loving partnership.

It was at this point that I started fretting about no longer being able to remember his voice and started cataloging our bedtime routines and endearments in my head in hopes of being able to hang onto the familiar phrases and cadences. I acknowledged:

> I even miss those little things I found irritating before—your tendency to let the coffee grounds build up in the machine without cleaning up before brewing a new pot, leaving debris in the sink instead of putting it down the disposal, taking more time than I had patience for to get some household and yard tasks done—but I'd give anything to get those irritations back again.

And I closed this entry by musing about the complex and confusing challenges ahead of me:

> I don't know if I can stand going on without you. No, that's not quite right. I have no intention of doing myself in, but I can't yet envision how to live alone again, though I know in my mind that this will become possible with the passage of time and commitment to the grief work that will enable me to honor your memory and find a new sense of "self" without you in my life. But my heart hasn't caught up with my head yet.
>
> My emotions feel all flattened out, and I understand that's quite "normal" for someone going through deep grieving, but sometimes it seems like I will never feel anything for anyone ever again. As soon as I commit those words to paper, I remember Maren and Trenton and how much I love those wonderful grand babies and how much you loved them, too. It makes me sad to think that they will never get to know their Papa, and how you will miss the excitement of watching them grow and change over time. I promise I will keep your memory present in their lives as much as possible. I'm dreading the morning since it should have been your birthday instead of the four-week anniversary of your death.

On November 7, the day that should have been a celebration of Skip's sixty-third birthday, I wrote of the humorous card I'd been saving for months, and the fact that Maren had made a homemade "princess" birthday card for him, and that I was going to put both in the memory book where I've been keeping various things that remind me of him. I explained that I'd spent some time talking with our lawyer, sorting through beneficiary information on his individual investments, and that I was expecting friends over for drinks on the deck, where "we intend to give you a birthday toast and celebrate your presence and our love for you, even though you are no longer here with us in the flesh."

The next morning, I gave credit to several friends, especially Zachary, and my grad school chum, Theresa, a working chaplain with terrific pastoral skills, for helping me endure yesterday's first major milestone day. I had shown Zachary the design of Skip's headstone, which he pronounced "just perfect," and Theresa had called to say that she and her family were so happy they had a chance to meet Skip the previous year and reinforced many of the things I was talking about with my grief counselor. I also told Skip that Kensey was having a hard time in her own grief, feeling unable to talk about it but wanting me to know she was thinking of me, and assuring him I thought it was healthier for her to express her grief rather than to keep things bottled up, as she had been doing at first. Kensey and I had the same tendency to tough it out in difficult circumstances, but my counselor's insistence on giving voice to my sorrow was starting to help me, and I hoped the same advice would help her, too.

The entries of the next couple of weeks were sharing the preparation and execution of his local memorial and telling him how Kensey and I had decided to give certain of his things to close friends and family members as well as the fact that we had decided to change our plans for Thanksgiving entirely and go visit Aunt Sue and Uncle Bill in North Creek instead of trying to replicate our usual holiday rituals without Skip or Tim's mom, who had also died earlier in the year.

During this same period, I found myself struggling with unexpected sexual longing. Our sex life had never been particularly robust due to challenges on both sides, though the lack had rarely bothered me while he was alive, but suddenly I missed sex—not sex in general, but sex with my husband. I expect this was a way to express how much I missed the physical contact between us because, in spite of the lack of regular sexual intimacy, we touched often and with great tenderness. Here's how I wrote about it some years later:

> After you died, I was never tempted in any serious way to look for a new partner in my life. It wasn't important for me at any time in the years following your death to look for romantic/ sexual satisfaction from anywhere: from another, from my own touch, or from my fantasies. And whenever I do fantasize about sex these days, it is almost always a kind of idealized memory of a passionate sexual relationship with you that never existed in real life, no matter how hard we tried. But there's never been any need to idealize the love we shared, even without the sexual bit. That was real, and when I think about it, I think of the intimate touch of bodies curling together skin to skin in complete comfort and with no need for sexual satisfaction to prove our delight in each other. I don't know if souls in the spirit world ever think about these kinds of human foibles, but I believe you'd agree with me about that joy.

All of these entries allowed me to unpack my own emotions in ways that, in retrospect, feel like an important part of my healing process. It was right before Thanksgiving that I admitted:

> I've been having a terrible time feeling motivated to write in this journal. It's not because I don't think of you all the time—I do, but I simply haven't felt like writing those thoughts down. I know I will probably regret this later when I try to recreate my feelings in these weeks after you died, but I can't help myself. . . . Thanksgiving is coming soon, and I'm having a hard time feeling thankful about much since you've been gone, but I am thankful for the wonderful life we had together, I'm thankful for the connections I've made with your family [especially those darling grandkids], and I'm thankful for friends who have made your

Thanksgiving at Aunt Sue's with Kensey, Tim, and kids.

passing, not bearable because it will never be that, but something approaching manageable for me.

On November 27, I wrote to assure Skip we had made the right choice to go to Bill and Sue's for Thanksgiving and how much fun we'd all had, but also described my own emotional meltdown in the middle of the night:

> The thing that's freaking me out right now is that for the most part the holiday has seemed entirely "normal," and I don't like it! There's something deeply wrong with that feeling, that sense of normal, since you've only been gone seven weeks, and the tears that came when that realization hit me were hard and hot. I could barely get my breath for the guilt and the grief. I know that we are all missing you—a lot—and perhaps that semblance of "normal" we all performed today was the desire not to grieve too much during what's supposed to be a time of good cheer

and thankfulness. But it still seems like some horrible mistake to me that I laughed and enjoyed myself quite a bit during the past two days. I know in my heart that you wouldn't want us to grieve forever, (but I've) lost my day-to-day companion, lover, and confidante, and the reality that brings to my life is something that I don't ever want to feel "normal" about, regardless of how many years pass by.

Between Thanksgiving and Christmas, I didn't journal as often as I had in the early weeks; in fact, I wrote only twice in three weeks until the Christmas entry itself. The events I wanted to tell Skip about were visiting the cemetery with his mom to put a holiday swag on his grave, keeping regular hours on campus (though I was not back to full-time teaching work yet), making Christmas plans with Kensey to visit them for nearly a week (the longest stay since just after the funeral), how Webster the cat has become such a comfort to me, and a surprising new job offer at the university that might be a good step for me to take. In the middle of this more mundane reporting, the more spiritual/psychological issues that preoccupied me were the same, especially wondering about the afterlife and what it signified for me.

Since first hearing folks at the wake talking about the reunion they imagined between Skip and Shirley, the issue of what happens after death has continued to niggle at me. I've never had a clear, spiritual sense of what happens to us after we die, nor did I ever feel its lack, but in grief, it returns from time to time. This time, it came in the middle of an imagined conversation between us on December 5 when visiting Skip's grave:

> I went by myself (to the cemetery) and had a long, tearful conversation with you. Though it was one-sided, I still felt comforted by being there, even though I couldn't stop crying once the floodgates opened. Did you see me there? Are you aware of me at all wherever it is you are? Or are you reunited with Shirley and happy there without me? I wish I could have some peace about this situation, since I would like to have the hope of joining you again in some future time and place, but I know I'll

never have an answer until I, too, am gone from this life. I guess I'll just have to learn to live with that particular ambiguity, won't I?

Almost two weeks later, on December 16, I mused about the so-called progress of my healing journey:

> There's an odd resistance starting to develop in me to the healing process: I don't really want to get over your loss, don't want to let go of this new identity. Daniel says he's pleased with my progress, and my work with Rebecca Rivers on yoga therapy and breathing is starting to make my body feel a bit more flexible and open. But I don't want to feel normal. I think that's probably why I'm still feeling quite emotionally flat. While I know that it's a natural part of the grieving process, I think it's also a kind of defense mechanism for me. I talked to Daniel a bit about the whole idea this afternoon, and he seemed to think that the guilt I felt about having a good time over Thanksgiving, which is part of this feeling, is also a very natural thing, given my circumstances. It's also true that grieving has given me an excuse to stop feeling like I have to be in control of everything all the time and has given me permission to be lazy, unfocused, and not my "usual" self. I wish I could have found a way in my life to get that release from the over-achiever identity without losing you to do it! I kept thinking it would happen when I was able to retire, and we could hang out together every day. But now, even when I retire, that hanging out during the day will be a different thing without you there.

It seems I put aside those concerns as the holidays approached, perhaps in hopes of avoiding any major "griefquakes" during this first Christmas as a solo woman once again, not by choice but by circumstance. I was still not comfortable identifying myself as a widow, even to myself. My final entry of 2010, made on the day after Christmas and eleven weeks after Skip's death, was sharing with him how the holidays had

Webster comes visiting with me for Christmas and makes a new friend.

unfolded for our little family group without him. It was a combination of descriptive narrative with a few reflections on my emotional state, and I suppose it was as much to remind myself of the event as anything else. I told him I had brought Webster with me and that he had been a big hit, especially with Maren. I narrated how she and I had made the Christmas Eve cookies for Santa and how her determination to learn everything, her constant "I do it" moments, had me convinced she would soon be taking over the Christmas baking on her own. Then I described how she helped us get ready for Santa:

> Even her Papa's death, which still affected her with acute sadness from time to time, couldn't dim her three-year-old enthusiasm for Santa's late-night arrival. Once everything was set up for Santa, we did a ritual of remembrance that Daniel had given to me in one of our sessions. I was glad that Kensey and Tim agreed to do it and that Maren wanted to help us. We set the candles up on a table in the living room, and then we read through the ritual words as each candle was lit. The first candle stood for our grief at our loss, the next for our courage in confronting our sorrow, then

for our memories of what you brought into our lives, and the final one for our love. Maren couldn't read yet, but in another "I do it" moment, she helped with lighting two sets of candles.

After the ritual, Maren cuddled with Kensey and Tim while Webster snuggled into my lap as we all sat in silence, remembering and missing you. Then it was time for hugs and kisses all around and for Maren to go to bed because "Santa only comes after everyone is asleep." We let the candles burn after that until the adults finally went to bed an hour or so later. I don't know if you are aware of anything that happens down here where we are all still muddling along, but I do hope you somehow know that you were missed.

Christmas morning had been exciting for Maren, and I tried to communicate that excitement to Skip the next day, saying I wished he could have been there to see her delivering presents to everyone and Trenton smiling and grabbing at interesting new things. I thought that everyone seemed happy with the holiday, even though the "elephant in the room" was the lack of his presence. Kensey and Tim gave me a cozy lap blanket with my initials embroidered on it, and I admitted that while there had been all sorts of good reasons for me to keep my own name when we got married, I now had a sense of wistfulness that there's no "S" on my blanket. Then I confided to Skip:

> I kept my emotions under control in front of others, but there were a couple of times that made me weepy. The first was early in the morning of my first day there when I got up to make the coffee and sit in the living room by myself. God, I missed you then! Webster, ever eager to soothe me, tried his best, snuggling and purring, but it just wasn't the same. The other one was when Kensey was putting Maren to bed on Christmas night, and it hit me hard just how much you would have loved all of these little moments. I ached for you so much I wasn't sure I could bear it. But then Kensey came out to tell me that Maren wanted me to come in her room for more hugs and kisses before she would go

to sleep, so I had to pull myself together. And it turns out that hugging a little heater girl just like her beloved Papa turned out to be very comforting for this grieving Gramma.

After Christmas, I stopped to visit Gloria on my drive home, showed her all the photos I had taken over the holiday visit, and took her over to the cemetery to visit Skip's grave. We rescued his evergreen swag from under the recent snowfall and made everything look really nice. She had a scarf over her lower face, so it was hard to tell her emotions, but I think she was having a tough time adjusting to his death. She hates displays of emotion, and she didn't say much to me that day, but I believe she appreciated that I wanted to visit the cemetery whenever I was in town, so I pledged to ask her to join me from now on. I closed the entry with this reflection: "Perhaps this time together at the cemetery will be the start of a new holiday tradition for both of us."

Returning to the journal in subsequent years, I found rereading these entries soothing, as if revisiting the early stages of this unanticipated journey could show me how far I had come during what felt like a remarkably difficult time.

I brought a wreath or swag to Skip's grave every holiday season for several years after his death.

CHAPTER TEN

NEW YEAR, NEW STRATEGIES

ON NEW YEAR'S Day, 2011, seventy-two days after Skip's death, six-and-a-half years since we first met in person, and five years, three months, and twenty-nine days since we committed our lives to each other, I entered a new calendar year without my beloved alive in it. I was still in what I called the reckoning stage of grief. This was not a coming to terms with my loss but rather a stage where everything was counted and put into my container of pain—where every anniversary of his passing, no matter how small, was noted and remarked on, each day and week was tallied as part of a trajectory of loss that I felt I needed to account for somehow. And yet I was finding occasional new ideas to wonder about in my journal on that day as well:

> Nearly a week has gone by since I've written in this journal, and
> I suspect that the gaps are likely to get longer and longer as my
> life starts finding its "new normal" patterns. Not that talking
> with you will get any less important; it's just that I might not be
> as likely to document those conversations that take place in my
> head, and perhaps less likely to report to you all the things that
> are happening to me. I don't know for sure, though. It's all so new
> and unwelcome, but sometimes this writing makes me feel like
> I'm clinging to you rather than honoring your memory by living
> my life in a way that would make you proud. I do hope you were
> present for all the holiday moments in some way, but I still don't

know for sure what I believe in that regard, even though there were times when I was sure I felt your presence with me.

Because we had recently done a ritual of remembrance on Christmas Eve, I decided to make another ritual of remembrance of my own for New Year's Eve. I would be spending that evening alone, and it would mark the passage from the last year of Skip's life to the first year since we met that I would have to live without the man I had come to love and trust. Describing that ritual made up an important piece of my morning journal on New Year's Day.

For the New Year's Eve ritual, I lit six candles for the six years we had together, placed a vase of flowers on the table alongside the large photo of Skip displayed at his funeral, because the garden and growing things had always been an important part of our bond, and planned on opening a bottle of our favorite Crémant de Bordeaux. To start things off, I read a poem that seemed to describe the flatness I'd been feeling since I came out of the initial shock of his death, in which the poet refers to the winter in his heart and wonders if spring will ever come again. And then, I started to talk with Skip about how I missed him, which led to a renewal of the keening and wailing in a way I hadn't done since the night he died. Once I had unburdened myself of those feelings, and the sobbing and tears had subsided, I opened the Crémant and poured us each a glass, setting his glass on the table with the photo, candles, and flowers as I drank and refilled my own over the course of the evening. I spent the rest of the evening going through our history together, using our many photo albums to remind me of how happy we had been and how many marvelous adventures we managed to pack into our short time together. The final thing I did—and I wasn't sure if I could face this when I started, but I managed—was to watch the DVD of our commitment ceremony, recording my response in my journal.

> You looked so handsome, and we looked so happy! It was heartbreaking to hear your voice (because I'm afraid I'm starting to forget what it sounds like) but a great comfort as well. I reiterated the vow we made to one another: "to love each other the only way I know how: completely and forever."

In addition to his funeral photo, this was another photo of Skip that I used to invoke his memory in some of my rituals that first year.

I must have slept well that night, for I woke refreshed and expected a low-key day since the usual holiday games were no longer anything I was planning to watch without my football aficionado beside me. I had been so occupied with the ritual that I made no New Year's resolutions, but Kensey must have done so because she called later in the day to talk to me about some things that happened right after Skip died that were still stressing her. We had a long, intense conversation, which was both incredibly difficult and remarkably good for both of us. We'd each said things to the other in grief in the last couple of months that the recipient was still carrying as tension. So we got them all out on the table, clarified what we meant, cried a lot, forgave each other, reaffirmed that we love each other, that we are still family even without our beloved patriarch, and that we plan for me to move near them when I retire. That evening, I explained the interaction to Skip:

> It was good for me to hear what was bothering her and to be able to express what was stressing me as well. I had never known how to broach some of the feelings that I was having, so once she started, I was able to say some important things about what had happened from my point of view and how I had been feeling about it. It seems I've said some things that have hurt her a great deal, and she has done the same to me. Now it's out there, and we've both realized that what we thought we were saying in the weeks after your funeral was not at all how the other person received the message, so the air has been cleared. We've promised each other to be more open about feelings and motivations (not easy for either of us), and I think the tensions are now moderated, if not eliminated. I'm feeling clear as I move into 2011. I know that might not last, since the sudden/unpredictable "grief attacks" are likely to reoccur for at least several months (and perhaps many more). It's impossible to know for sure, but I do feel like I made a significant emotional leap forward in the last couple of days.

It was more than a week before I wrote in the journal again, and on January 9, the three-month anniversary of his death, it seemed like I was already anticipating the beginning of the end of this journaling strategy for managing my grief.

> It seems less urgent now for me to write to you all the time, since I've started talking with you directly each day: telling you what's going on for me in mundane and minute detail the way I used to do all the time when you were here to listen in person. I don't think I've ever had such a wonderful and attentive listener in my entire life, and I miss that so much, but now I've started telling the air and hoping you are still present enough in the ether around me to hear my stories.

Today marks three months since you left this earth, and it still seems unreal to me most of the time. I keep expecting to turn over in bed during the night and find you there, to hear your voice, to see you sitting at your computer or coming around the corner any minute now. My head knows this is not possible, but my heart still has not caught up . . . may never catch up to what I know intellectually to be true.

I went on to admit that I worried my ongoing desire to write about my grief on Facebook, especially the tribute I had just put there for the three-month anniversary, might be distressing to Kensey. I imagined she might not want to be reminded of the loss, feeling that she had to put aside her own grief because of other more immediate concerns, especially her job and the kids. I also admitted that I was thinking I should perhaps moderate my public expression of feelings for her sake but without suppressing them entirely.

I also shared with Skip that my grief counselor, Daniel, had told me that I'd been grieving in a healthy and productive way, for which he was very proud of me:

> He validates my progression along this difficult road, reminds
> me that it is a very long process (and that your sudden loss
> is still counted in mere days), and that there is no reason to
> ever feel obliged to "get over it" and move on. His advice and
> encouragement have been invaluable to me in these past three
> months. I know I'm stepping into a new phase of grief, though,
> not because it's been a particular length of time, but because
> the holidays, while very difficult, were also cathartic (thanks to
> the rituals), and I feel I'm ready to start carefully and mindfully
> stepping back into the larger world. Until now, I've been cautious
> and have stayed protected within the confines of close friends,
> neighbors, and family. Going back to work and starting to become
> a full participant in my professional life again will expand my
> horizons, and I think I'm ready for that. . . . This feels like new
> territory, and I'm a new person, so I will have to be articulate

about that to be sure people don't expect me to be my old self again, at least not right away. Daniel reminded me that when people ask me how I'm doing, it's not smart to simply say, "I'm fine," because then people will start making demands on me that might cause even more stress. I'm planning a different answer: "I'm doing the best I can and just taking things one day at a time."

Daniel also reminded me that I didn't have to like it—I just had to get through it. I ended this entry with a detailed report on my new daily routine around the house. Something about finding that routine and sharing it felt important to me at the time, though the details were predictably mundane, including whether I would read the morning paper before or after doing my morning yoga and feeding the cat. In the past, I have often claimed that I was a creature of rhythm and that once I found the patterns and pacing of any new situation, such as a job change or new creative endeavor, I could become comfortable with it. I guess it was true about grieving, too.

Almost a week later, on January 14, what I wrote was again full of the minutiae of my new routines, now including details about my time at the office since I was officially back to work. I'm aware of the privilege afforded me as an academic with a long winter break where nothing was expected of me, and as a middle-class woman living in a rural small town with a strong personal support system, and I feel blessed that I was given the needed time to deal with my loss. I know this is not the case for everyone. Writing was still one of my ways to find solace, though it was no longer a daily routine. Sharing those details with Skip through the journal gave me something to do in the evening when I would rather have been telling him all about it in person. I focused on course prep and my thoughts about returning to the classroom very soon. I also shared the news about the new administrative job I'd accepted and how others had been so supportive of my decision in that regard. I also told Skip in detail about the planner I'd retained to help with all the financial details surrounding the will, our real estate "empire," my retirement planning, and all the other details that he would normally have been taking care of for both of us. I closed this long explanation of the particulars of my last several days with another musing about the more spiritual aspects of his passing that still confounded me, though somewhat less so as time continued to pass:

> I wish you were still here, but I know intellectually there's nothing I can do to change the reality that you will never be with me in the flesh again. I'm still more than a little confused about whether or not we will be reunited in some other world when I eventually pass over, but at the moment I don't think that's going to be happening any time soon, so I try not to think about it too much. In the meantime, I must content myself with your presence in the prisms and the photos, with your beautiful, furry namesake, and with remembering the many wonderful times we did have together. That way, I can keep you alive in my heart.

Three silent weeks later, on February 6, I got around to reporting in-depth that returning to the classroom was easier than I had feared it might be, but my biggest challenge had actually been coming home at the end of the workday to a cold, empty house. I shared the details of how I had fixed most of those issues—by keeping NPR on all day, using light timers, and having a new programmable thermostat installed—so the house would be light, warm, and filled with noise when I arrived. I also praised Webster, who was always waiting faithfully each day for me to return, acting more like a dog than a cat, though it was more likely to be separation anxiety than temperament, given his history of being abandoned in the past. Though trivialities took up most of the page, there were still a few emotional outbursts, including this report of a recent meltdown in yoga class:

> This week will mark four months since your heart stopped forever. I've been taking yoga classes for a few weeks now, and two classes ago, I had a bit of a meltdown during śavāsana. My teacher was coaching the meditation and asked us to become aware of our chests, inside and out, and suddenly I couldn't stop thinking about how your heart had stopped, and I couldn't stop

Webster was my sustaining companion in those early months.

crying. The breathing is supposed to get easier with awareness, but unfortunately when one is crying, breathing isn't very smooth.

And I'm starting to cry now because I still can't quite believe that you're not here. Even though my head accepts that it's true, my heart keeps on hoping for some kind of miracle, for me to somehow awaken from the nightmare and laugh about it all with you.

I had started to notice a great deal of repetition in my journal entries; some of the phrases were reappearing almost verbatim because I had run out of new ways to express the issues that continued to press in on me, though I also noticed that I had less need to use writing to feel better. My grief was diminishing in small but palpable ways, though I was still not ready to let go of it yet. Because both work and daily life routines were starting to find their own new rhythms, it was two months before I wrote in my journal again, though I never stopped thinking about Skip or the things I would have told him if he were with me in person. On April 8, I disclosed that I had appeared as a guest speaker in Daniel's graduate class in "Death, Dying, and Bereavement" to share my experience of Skip's death with students who were studying to be school counselors, and that I felt it had been worthwhile, both for me and for the students to have that discussion. I also admitted that I was finally starting to think about what to do in the yard this year, though this had initially presented me with an unexpected challenge, one that I identified as "Spring is a bitch without you":

> I find I write to and about you less and less these days. But it doesn't mean I think about you any less. In fact, if anything I think about you more often, and I talk to you in my head or out loud every day as well. Perhaps it's that I've internalized this conversation so thoroughly that I don't want or need to write much of anything down anymore. One thing I found thought-provoking is the surprise I felt when spring came. I believed that the return of spring and the light would lift my spirits, but it had exactly the opposite effect. I was blindsided by spring because it seemed so fucking unfair that everything around me was coming back to life, but you were still gone. I was depressed for days about that.

After assuring Skip I had the gardening under control now, with the help of a friend of his, as well as Toby and Debbie, who had purchased a lovely memory tree for my garden, I closed with the acknowledgment that the next day, April 9, would be the six-month anniversary of his death and wondered what the day might bring:

> It could be a "regular" day, or it could be a tough one to get through. These anniversaries are unpredictable, and I feel like this

Thanks to Toby and Debbie, this tricolor beech was planted in Skip's memory where his veggie garden used to be.

one could be a big one. . . . especially since it's another Saturday and it's supposed to be sunny, just like it was the Saturday you died. I'm hoping that I'll be surrounded by my prisms all day. They make me feel like I'm being encompassed in your embrace somehow. There are no words to say how much I wish this could be literally true, and I know that's impossible. But they comfort me anyway.

This turned out to be the last formal entry in what I call my grief journal, though I continued to write about my loss and my grief journey in other formats. Most of that work ended up in this memoir. I did continue to have regular internal conversations with Skip, especially as I got nearer to my retirement and moving out of the house he and I had shared and down to western Massachusetts nearly four years after his death to be near our grandkids. In fact, more than thirteen years later, these conversations in my head haven't stopped. I have learned to move ahead with my life, though I will never call it "moving on," which implies that I'm done with mourning Skip's loss. That grief will be with me in some form or other for the rest of my life, no matter what else might happen in the future.

CHAPTER ELEVEN

EARLY MILESTONES
(THE FIRST FEW YEARS)

AFTER I STOPPED writing regularly in my grief journal, I kept on writing, and what I wrote had a new, different format. By then, I knew I would write this grief memoir. Each of the shorter pieces were about experiences I had during my ongoing mourning, but they didn't fit the format of the overarching narrative I had been crafting for the story of Skip and Rebecca. They were shorter and more focused on specific emotional memories and challenges. These experiences or thoughts that grief delivered to me over time didn't hang together in a traditional narrative way, and they were not designed to be self-help advice for others. They were simply important milestones in my grief journey—intimate elements of my widow story—and I decided to share them. The result is the next two chapters, where these short essays are shared in a more or less chronological order.

PERSONAL GRIEVING RITUALS
(from November 7, 2010, to the present)

Grief rituals are the things we do to self-soothe when certain things remind us of our loss. Being a theatre person, at first, I created rituals that were more elaborate and formal, often involving candles, incense, photos, wine, music, and even speaking, though prepared words were few. For

This was a setup for one of the more elaborate rituals I created in the first year after Skip's death.

Skip's birthday, which came only three and a half weeks after his death, I set up a small altar with his photograph, played his favorite music, toasted him with a glass of Bordeaux (one of our favorite wines and reminiscent of our trip to that city in France some years back), and spoke to him from my heart about how much I missed him. I did similar rituals for many of the important "firsts" without him in the year after his death.

In my daily life, I also created several smaller, more informal rituals, and though they have decreased in emotional impact as time passes, they will always help me remember certain things that I loved and still love. I remember thinking immediately after Skip died that I would never be able to count to ten again in the same way, because I lost the love of my life on the ninth day of the tenth month. I was right about that. Anything that required linear, mathematical thinking, and often things that didn't, had me counting to ten in my head, saying, "I lost him on the ninth day of the tenth month" (instead of "nine, ten"). I counted the ice cubes I grabbed to fill a glass for a cocktail or iced tea, the crackers I pulled out of the box for a snack, how many seconds I would gargle after brushing my teeth, the number of times I ran the lip balm over my mouth, even how many spoonfuls of yogurt I would have for breakfast straight from the carton since I no longer needed to bother with a bowl. I started to count anything and everything. At first it was obsessive—any excuse to count to ten—and even now, more than thirteen years later, it still enters my mind now and then when I do the things I used to count in the early months after Skip's death.

I also have a continuing relationship with the prismatic light that had bathed Skip's body in what seemed like an otherworldly glow when I found him unresponsive in his chair. Those prisms had been created by the sun shining through an antique beveled, stained-glass window that hung near his favorite chair in our old home. It was then transplanted to the dining room of my new home near the kids a few years

Once the window was hung in the new house, prisms visited often on sunny days. This day, they are visiting the sideboard that was one of the first pieces of furniture we bought together.

later. Whenever the sun creates those prisms on the walls and furniture, I always greet them as an embodiment of his spirit in my house, a house he's never been inside in the flesh. I will often touch the wall where the prisms shine, letting the light play on my hands, and say, "Hi, Sweetie, it's good to see you."

When he was alive, in addition to being a consummate bartender, Skip was also the housemaid because while I was still working full-time, he had taken early retirement. That meant he was the one who did our laundry. I had one pair of comfortable cotton undies that had black polka dots on a white background, and he insisted they were his favorites, not because they were sexy but because the design let him know without having to put on his glasses when they came from the dryer inside out and needed to be turned to the right side before being folded and put away in the drawer. Yes, my husband folded the laundry! For the first several years after his death, whenever there was a family event or a special occasion I felt he would have enjoyed, I would wear those undies.

And last, but not least, there is the bartender's signature cocktail: the Manhattan. It was always his favorite. Made with Canadian or rye whiskey, sweet vermouth, bitters, and a cherry, it's still my cocktail of choice any time I want to feel Skip's energy with me or think about a decision I would have consulted him over if he were still around to advise me, especially in matters of finance or investment, which had been one of his special talents. And sometimes for no reason that I can discern, I just need to pour myself a Manhattan to feel closer to him, counting out ten ice cubes in the process.

CHALLENGES WITH A NEW CAT AND YOGA BREATHING
April 30, 2011
(Six months and three weeks after)

Ujjayi Pranayama is the primary breathing practice of Svaroopa yoga. It's also called "ocean-sounding" breath, because you use a slight tension in the throat muscles to be able to hear your own inhale and exhale.

According to my yoga teacher, regular breathing practice would help me with general health as well as my asthma-challenged breathing. I already had issues with not being able to get a good breath because of asthma, but after Skip died, my body folded in on itself and my chest seized up in such a way that it was like having a vise tightened around my ribs. I always felt winded, even when I wasn't exerting myself. My grief counselor suggested that because my heart was broken, my upper body was probably tensing around it in an instinctive drive to protect me. It didn't feel like protection at all, though. It felt like a threat to my well-being. So about two months after his death, and after several private yoga therapy sessions to help my body unclench itself and learn to relax again, I started practicing Ujjayi Pranayama for twenty minutes a day, managing to average at least five and sometimes six days a week.

Other than the usual struggles with sustaining a daily practice of anything, I discovered that there were two unique challenges I encountered as I did my Ujjayi breathing: one physical, one emotional. I had a guided practice track copied from a CD to my iPod, so Swami Nirmalananda, the founder and master teacher of Svaroopa yoga, coached me through my twenty minutes each day. I propped my legs up on a blanket stack and blocks, put another folded blanket under my head, and covered myself with yet another blanket. I used a lavender-scented eye pillow to cover my eyes, which helped me focus internally. As you can imagine, it took quite an effort to get into position before turning on the iPod, relaxing, and beginning a meditative focus on the breath. Once I'd gotten started, I didn't like to be interrupted.

My first test was, simply put, my cat Webster. When I first started the Ujjayi breathing practice, Webster would curl up on a little Tibetan rug I had in the room where I do my yoga . . . or sometimes on my chair. However, in the last several weeks he has decided that he really loves the new blanket I use to cover myself. But he doesn't just want to cuddle on it. Once I get under my blanket and ready to start, he climbs up on my propped legs, straddles one of my legs, starts to bite my toes, and humps my leg! At first, I tried to stay as still as possible in hopes that he would stop, but he's been hanging on longer and longer. I have now proven that I am more determined than he is persistent, but those first several minutes are quite challenging for my concentration. Prior to this experience, I thought only dogs had the urge to hump human legs, but I was wrong! The internet tells me that one possible reason why neutered male cats hump blankets is because they're needy for affection, which doesn't make sense to me, since Webster gets more cuddle time than any other cat I've ever had. But it can also happen when they want your attention, and he's no longer getting my attention when I'm focusing on my breathing.

The second challenge isn't physical; it's emotional. It comes when, near the end of the practice, my guiding voice on the iPod asks me to look deeper into my breathing process, as she always does at a fixed point in the practice. She coaches me to concentrate on the subtle movement in my chest that happens before, during, and after the oxygen starts to flow as I breathe in and out. She identifies this movement as prana, calls it "the non-breath breath," and identifies it as the life force underlying all breath. Every time this moment in the practice comes, I find myself wondering about what it was like for Skip as his prana left him and he stopped breathing forever—when "the non-breath breath" became a literal rather than figurative phenomenon. Did awareness of what was happening come to him when his heart stopped, or did he pass quietly into something like sleep, not realizing what was really going on? Or was it something else entirely, something that we who are still living can't comprehend?

The first time this thought occurred to me was in a yoga class, and it hit me like a sudden blow that knocks the wind out of your lungs. I started gasping for breath and crying—intensely, profoundly—but silently, so it passed for deep yoga breathing and no one noticed that something different was happening to me. These days there are no longer any sudden tears; just an intense longing to understand something I'll never be able to know until it happens to me. I suppose it's as good a subject as any for my next meditation.

MUSINGS ON MUSCLE MEMORY AND MARRIAGE
January 10, 2013
(Three years and three months after)

Muscle memory, which the dictionary defines as "the ability to reproduce a particular movement without conscious thought, acquired as a result of frequent repetition of that movement," is a pretty amazing thing. Just when my mind thinks that I'm adjusting to being a widow, my body betrays me with a memory so visceral I can't ignore it. Last night in the middle of the night, I got up to pee. This is not an uncommon occurrence for women, especially of my age. When I climbed back into bed half asleep, I slid backward under the covers with my body curled up, expecting to be spooned by the other warm body in the bed, a body that would always curl around me and hold me, regardless of how sound asleep its owner had been mere moments before. But he wasn't there. My mind already knew it, but my body forgot, and as a result I came fully awake suddenly, sobbing with the renewed shock of absence and loss.

I'm not one to go find myself a new warm body, any body, to replace the one I lost. This is why I spent almost twenty years living alone and mostly celibate after my divorce, with only a couple of affairs, both of them before I turned forty. Then Skip came along when I was in my menopausal mid-fifties and transformed my world. It would have to be a special person to jolt me out of the memory of the remarkable marriage we had. Because I found a way to negotiate a two-year paid research leave from my teaching work as a university professor, and because we were able to orchestrate those two years so that we could be together much of every single day, we had more time in each other's immediate presence than many working couples who've been together for a decade or more.

My first marriage, when I was in my late twenties and early thirties, lasted nearly eight years before our divorce was final, but we were living apart for almost three of those years. Even in the early years of the marriage, I was at work for many hours every day, especially after I founded and started to run a small theatre company and evening rehearsals started to become a regular part of my job. My second marriage was different from the first. It had all the wonderful aspects of a long marriage without having to go through all the ups and downs of growing up together that I believe happened to couples like my parents and others who married young and perhaps even raised a family together. When you meet and marry in your fifties, it's easier to bypass some of the growing pains younger folks might experience. The only regret Skip ever voiced to me in our time as a couple was that because of our age we weren't able to have children of our own, though we did have a treasured young friend who was like a son to us. And we had two grandchildren, which was and is a blessing that I had never expected to experience, and one that sustains me as I continue my life without him. Another blessing is that in our blended families, no one has ever thought to differentiate between the step-grandparents and the biological ones.

This second marriage—the one I can't let go of yet—lasted just over six years from first meeting to sudden unexpected parting, but that relationship was a true marriage in all the best senses of the word. Even as my mind gets used to the identity of "widow" and learns to get through most days without emotional backsliding, my body continues to struggle. And it isn't always big moments, either. Another surprising place where muscle memory plays a part in an occasional grief eruption has been the changing of sheets on the bed. It's much different doing it alone, because it was something we always did together, and my body often forgets about that, too.

I used to joke with Skip that I had two women to thank for the success—and even the circumstances that created the possibility—of our marriage: Shirley, his deceased first wife, who trained him well in the ways of the household and from whom he learned (or with whom he practiced—this could have been his own innate nature as well) extraordinary love and loyalty; and Marcia, the woman he dated after Shirley's death, who first brought him to the north country and then kicked him to the curb several months before he and I first met. I used to tease that if I were to die suddenly, he would have been married again within two years. He denied it, but I know there are some who need to be partnered to survive, some who are compelled to live single, and others who can go either way, depending on the circumstances. He was of the first category; I am of the latter. I've experienced the marriage of my dreams, and I feel no urgent need to look for a replacement, even though my body still aches in memory of what I have lost. My muscles will never let me forget.

ONLINE GRIEVING BRINGS HELPFUL CONNECTIONS
2010 to 2015
(The first five years)

Because I was too exhausted and discombobulated to send notices about Skip's death to extended family members and far-away friends, I posted information about it on Facebook the morning after it happened, which brought an avalanche of responses from friends (including some I hadn't heard from since high school), former students, and even professional acquaintances. At first, it was a simple shortcut, a convenient way to get word to family and friends who weren't local, but then it became a kind of lifeline for me that kept me connected, however tenuously, to the larger world. In those first months, it was easy to become isolated in my grief-infused routines, but the feedback I was getting on Facebook and in email correspondence helped keep me from falling off the map entirely. So, I kept on posting every few days, mostly because I didn't have the energy to make more personal contact with anyone but those in my most immediate circle of family and friends in those early days. And so many people seemed to want to know how I was doing. Best of all, it kept me talking—giving voice to my sorrow, as my grief counselor had advised—even though I was not yet up to seeing many people in person.

I have often said that Facebook saved my life during the deepest hours of my grief because it brought me support from afar and didn't have to be dealt with on anyone's timeline but my own, which was often in the middle of the night when sleep wouldn't come. I was incapable of knowing what I wanted or needed and was isolated unless close friends dropped by to see me, often unannounced. Like Zachary: "Hi, I'm walking the dog, do you feel like joining? No pressure." Or Diane: "I'm on my way to the store; can I bring you anything?" The many other friends who said, "Call if you need anything, day or night," never heard from me because I had no idea what I needed, other than to wake from this dreadful dream and find my husband still alive. Denial was a big part of my widow experience in the early weeks—hoping it was all a bad dream, even in the face of evidence that it wasn't and that I was, in fact, all alone in my house. My house . . . no longer our house. That my love was not going to return to rejoin me there.

After several months, I became aware of a number of online grieving groups. In the beginning, I just skulked around the edges, lurking without engaging in the conversations, checking out what other widowed people were saying about their situations. Eventually, I took the plunge and joined a Facebook group called Widownet, focusing on conversations that had the most meaning for me and the people who said the things that resonated most comfortably. On its main website, Widownet, established in 1995, identifies itself as "the first online information and self-help resource for, and by, widows and widowers. Topics covered include grief, bereavement, recovery, and other information helpful to people, of all ages, religious backgrounds, and sexual orientations, who have suffered the death of a spouse or life partner."

I wasn't looking for comfort. I wanted conversation with people who understood this experience of losing a loved partner because no matter how loving and supportive my in-person friends were, there were some things they just didn't understand—because it had never happened to them. Yet. I'm a teacher, and reading is as normal for me as breathing, so I followed certain conversations, now and then using the "like" button to indicate agreement, but never adding my own two cents' worth. I also investigated other FB grief groups but never entered conversations there, either. I kept returning to Widownet and started to recognize a few names, mostly of women who seemed to be struggling in ways similar to my own. After several months, I decided to join a couple of conversations that interested me, especially conversations about the afterlife, where I had my most serious spiritual issues. I even started a couple of queries in hopes of getting a conversation started about what people think happens to us after death. I laid out my dilemma about the possibility of reunion in the afterlife because my husband had a deceased first wife before meeting me. The first thing I encountered was the animosity of several newly widowed women who did not want to hear anything about possible alternatives to being reunited with their lost husbands in some imagined afterlife. When I asked about what someone who married another widowed person could expect if reunion was the ultimate goal, that brought even more negativity. But it also brought me a few new allies who were struggling with similarly ambiguous issues in adjusting to widowhood. In the process of having a few side conversations, we realized that the real difference was not in our spiritual beliefs but more to do with the timing of the loss. Everyone who was struggling with large existential questions was several months or even a couple of years into their widowed lives, and the loudest antagonists were the newly widowed who needed comfort, not questions, and absolute answers, not maybes or what-ifs.

Eventually, a small group of about ten like-minded new friends left Widownet and formed our own Facebook group. There were also bumps in that road as a few early members never engaged in the conversation, which had been the goal of the smaller group—to discourage lurkers— and those folks dropped off quickly. Eventually, the group settled to just four women who, though widely separated by geography and life experiences, were all at a similar place in our grief journeys, and we enjoyed having very deep conversations about our grieving processes over the course of two years. Issues we discussed included anniversaries; unexpected grief surges (aka "griefquakes"); reactions of others to our grieving (especially those we identified as toxic friends or family members); the challenges of finding or going back to work; financial challenges; health challenges (especially having to deal with them alone) and therapy experiences; transitions (especially moving away from the house shared with the deceased spouse); and much more. It wasn't all serious, though. We also discussed our pets' antics (we all had them) and the pleasures we experienced in our daily lives, no matter how small. We also shared milestones when we felt good about our abilities to handle challenging situations that would have been easy for us, if not for the grief.

We had our share of differences over time, and after a couple of dramatic blowups and reconciliations, the group dissolved as a unit. We all remain FB friends years later, though it's a club we all wished we'd never had to become part of in the first place. There are in-person grief groups in many communities, but each of us felt more comfortable doing this kind of intimate sharing online, and most of us lived in small, isolated, rural communities where going online was a more acceptable approach than driving a long distance. For me, this group provided support for what I think of as the middle years of my grief process. I was eager to go online to see what my friends were thinking about, and they heard my worries and my triumphs without judgment and with great understanding of the emotional challenges. It was yet another lifeline, and while I imagine an online experience is not for everyone, mine helped me stay centered and feel balanced as I re-entered first my existing and then—a few years later—my new community while navigating such a profound loss and dramatic change in my identity and long-term plans. I owe a great debt of gratitude to these women.

CHAPTER TWELVE

FARTHER DOWN
THE ROAD
(LATER YEARS)

IN ADDITION TO the early experiences, I also wrote several short pieces that reflect other grieving-related experiences over longer periods of time, including some good travel memories, a lifelong affinity for cemeteries (not always shared by other members of Skip's family), and an emotional situation that affected me years after his death. I continued to display photos of my guy all over my house to the point that folks who were just getting to know me would ask about who he was and wonder when they might get to meet him. Then I would tell them my story. I've heard that some people no longer display photos of their deceased loved ones because the images remind them of the absence and make them too sad. For me, it's just the opposite. I crave those reminders and find it remarkable how photographic memories can bring back a person's essence, even though they are no longer in the room with you.

REMEMBERING TRAVELS WITH THE
GEEZER MODEL
(Before and After)

After the first harrowing courtship year, when most of our travels were related to medical issues (his and my mother's), Skip and I traveled to many places together for pleasure in the US, Canada, and even one trip

On our trip to visit friends in France and Ireland. This is on the deck of a tea shop in Dingle.

to France, England, and Ireland to visit friends and family in those countries. In fact, the only trip during our time together that he didn't want to join me on was one I made to India. Our house was new at the time, and I suspect that feeling a need to stay home after all the medical travel of the previous year was part of the reason for his reluctance.

We took a seven-week cross-country driving trip the year after our commitment ceremony and called it our honeymoon: driving west across Canada through every province except Quebec and the Maritimes, down the western coast of the US (with stops to visit family and friends in Oregon and northern California), then cutting inland through central California toward the desert Southwest with sightseeing stops in many national and tribal parks (from Yosemite and Death Valley in California; to Sedona/Red Rocks, Grand Canyon, Canyon de Chelly, and Monument Valley in Arizona; to Bryce and Zion in Utah; to Mesa Verde and Garden of the Gods in Colorado) and many other tourist sites in the region (including stops in Santa Fe and Taos in New Mexico), followed by a long, diagonal, almost nonstop drive back to our home in northern New York.

The geezer model near the top of Banff Mountain, calling to wish Kensey a happy birthday, which we missed because of our cross-country driving adventure.

Most days our travels involved moderate drives, prearranged hotel stays in a chain that provided free hot breakfasts, a cooler full of lunch fixings deployed at various rest stops along the way, and (of course the bartender would have thought of this) a bar bag for our evening Manhattans once we arrived at our hotel and found the ice machine. Some days our drives were more leisurely than others, involving stops along the way, and many photos were taken, earning Skip his second enduring nickname—the geezer model—because of his cheerful willingness to be a regular subject in many of those photos.

Prior to the proliferation of cell phones and sharing one's every move on Facebook, I circulated photos of our trip via email. I narrated our trip and captioned all the photos I shared. Because taking one's own photo with an SLR digital camera required a tripod and self-timer, I made Skip serve as my photo model at least once in each location. At first, I just used his name. Then I switched to "that handsome fellow" because he was in so many photos, always good-natured and smiling. It was just a week into our long drive when I first started referring to Skip in a photo at a scenic overlook in Banff National Park (in Alberta, Canada) as the "by-now-famous geezer model."

These travel narrations and photo captions started turning into email conversations with friends who were following us on the journey, and Skip's new nickname was well received. Two days after the first use of his new moniker, in captions for photos we took of each other in the beautiful gardens at Stanley Park in British Columbia, I started calling myself "the geezer girl" since I was the companion of "that famous geezer model." When we ferried from Canada to the US through the San Juan Islands, I was calling him "the internationally famous geezer model," and by the time we made it to Golden Gate Park in San Francisco, around the halfway mark in our travels, I was calling him "the infamous geezer model," undoubtedly because of comments from friends about his previous photos. He continued to be the centerpiece of my photo essays through the desert Southwest. These regular photo appearances turned out to be a great comfort to me in the months and years after his death. Photos of our many travels continue to keep him alive in my memory and to remind me what a copacetic travel companion I had in Skip.

He also accompanied me when I presented at summer academic conferences, so we saw Chicago and New Orleans together, as well as coastal Connecticut, where I was a special faculty guest at the Eugene O'Neill Theatre Center. And, of course, we went often to visit family and friends for both joyous and sad occasions, including when my mother died and when each of our two grandchildren were born. We were looking forward to much more travel together and had booked a cross-country sleeper car train trip from New York to Oregon for a nephew's high school graduation just a week before Skip's death. These days, instead of traveling with the geezer model, I often travel to the geezer model to visit his grave, and whenever I take a trip of any length,

The now-internationally-famous geezer model and his geezer girl visit Stonehenge.

I always imagine how his presence would soothe and encourage me. The thing that continues to bring a dull ache all these years later when planning any new trip is that there are no longer photos of the geezer model to add to my albums when I return home.

CEMETERY VISITS
(Before it happened and long after)

I have always loved cemeteries. My first real memories of visiting cemeteries happened long before I knew anyone who was buried there. On Sunday morning when I was a kid, Mom would sometimes decide it was a good time to go "mushrooming," one of her favorite hobbies, so we would all set out for the cemetery she considered primo territory for finding meadow mushrooms, which were just like the ones most other people bought in the grocery store. Here they were free for the picking. My father died when I was twenty-three, and Mom had a bench installed near his grave in that same cemetery, so she could visit Dad with a picnic lunch in hand. From then on, she modeled for me the idea of visiting the dead and communing with them, even years after they have left this world, an idea that appealed to me, both then and now. The cemetery was also a great place to walk the dog, which was another thing Mom loved to do, especially in all the years of living alone with only her canine companions after Dad died. I know some people find cemeteries creepy because of the proximity to the incontrovertible evidence of death, but I have always found them more relaxing than scary, and in the case of this particular cemetery, extraordinarily beautiful, especially in the spring when the azaleas, rhodies, and flowering trees were all in bloom.

After Skip died, it was the most natural thing in the world for me to visit his grave. The challenge was that the Stoughton family plot where he is buried between his father and his first wife, and where I will join him one day, was a three-hour drive away from where I was living and working right after his death. The cemetery is very close to where my mother-in-law, Gloria, lived in her retirement community, so I was able to visit her whenever I wanted to make the drive, which I did about

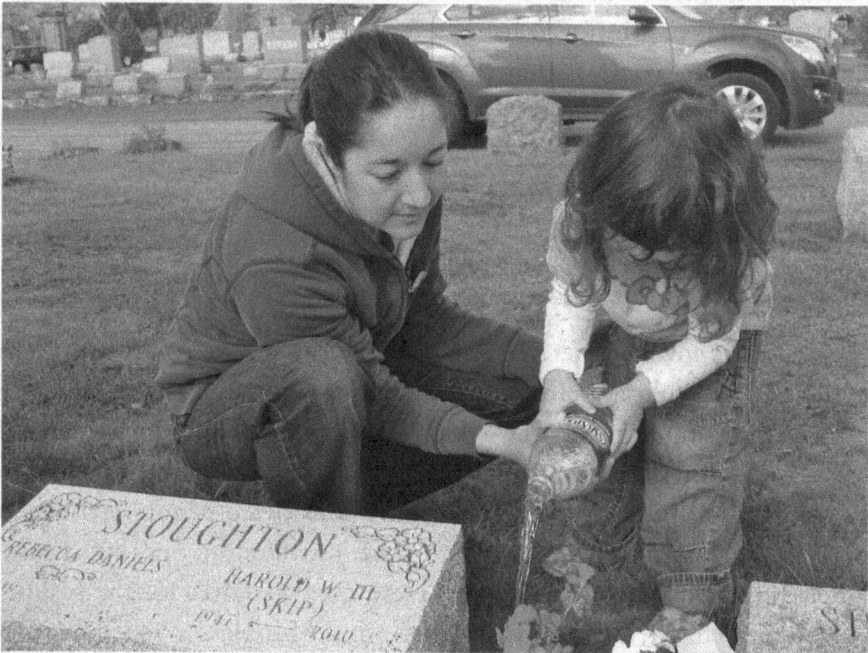

Visiting Skip's grave with Kensey and Maren who helped me water the flowers planted by the gravestone.

every four to six weeks in those first few years after his death. Gloria was the self-appointed cemetery caretaker for the Stoughton clan, so at first, she always went with me when I visited Skip. She would brush off her husband's gravestone while I looked after Skip's stone, checked the perennial flowers that had been planted after Shirley's death many years before, and tended the windchimes I had installed near Skip's headstone a couple of years after his death. My brother-in-law Scott had a job working for the county with juvenile offenders, and he often took a work crew to the cemetery to help with general cleanup, so I always let him know when I left something on Skip's grave—a mum plant in the fall, a wreath at Christmastime, a pot of annuals in the spring or summer—and he would make sure to keep an eye on the plants and dispose of the spent wreath. After Gloria went into nursing care and could no longer join me on my cemetery visits, I still stopped by to see her before every visit to the cemetery, but then I would often grab a sandwich and, just as my mother used to do, bring my lunch to Skip's grave and eat it there, using a camp chair I kept in my car. Now and then, if they were able to come to town, I might have lunch with Kensey's Aunt Sue and Uncle Bill, who had become my good friends as well.

Four years after Skip's death, I retired to western Massachusetts to be near Kensey, Tim, and the grandkids, which made the drive to the cemetery only about two hours, though it was still a half-day commitment. I kept up the visiting routine with a stop to see Gloria, or lunch with Bill and Sue at a local restaurant, or sandwich lunch at the cemetery for the next several years, and the visits chatting with Skip in the cemetery started to get shorter and the intervals between visits started to get longer as time passed, though there was always one visit in every season of the year. Eventually, my mother-in-law and brother-in-law both died, and Bill and Sue were not doing as much driving as they had in years past, so more often than not, my visit was directly to the cemetery after a quick stop to pick up some lunch.

Then the pandemic put a wrench in everyone's plans. The first time I tried to visit the cemetery a few weeks after the first lockdown was declared in the Northeast, I was able to enter stores masked, but many of the restrooms I counted on during my drive were not open. I did manage to make the drive, ate the quickest lunch ever (skipping the beverage), and completed the return drive without having to find a place in the woods along the road to pee. It had now been almost ten years since Skip had died, so I decided that perhaps I didn't need to visit the cemetery as often, especially while the pandemic raged and no living relatives were there to visit, concluding that once or twice a year was enough. And I felt his presence in my home when the sunlight hit the prisms more often than I ever did while visiting his grave.

Recently, Kensey and Tim were able to realize their long-held dream of buying a summer cottage on Lake Cossayuna, not too far from Fort Edward. This was a place Kensey had visited in her childhood, and she and Tim bought it from extended family members. So, of course, I visited them at the lake. On my way home, I decided to go over to Fort Edward to visit the cemetery for the first time in many months. As I pulled into the cemetery lanes, a thunderstorm erupted in the sky above me, so I ate my takeaway meal in the car, enjoying the sound of the rain pounding down and telling Skip all about the kids' new lake cottage. When the rain finally stopped, I was greeted with a beautiful rainbow over the view to the east of the cemetery. I saw traces of that arch for the first part of my drive home and felt like Skip's spirit was in that prismatic bow in the sky, giving me permission not to visit as often in the future and guiding me home.

FAREWELL TO WEBSTER
Summer 2021 (Almost eleven years after)

I got my cat, Webster, less than two weeks after Skip died, naming him in memory of the man who would have loved that big, friendly, ginger cat but whom he would never meet: Harold Webster Stoughton III. A mellow, almost five-year-old who had been surrendered to the shelter when his family moved out of the area and was unable to take him along, Webster was my constant companion in those first few weeks when all I could do was sit in a recliner and stare at nothing. Sometimes, I had enough energy to read or to post something online, and now and then a friend would drop in to check on how I was doing. They would almost always find me in one of our several recliners with the orange fuzzball on my lap or stretched out on my legs.

Though one could never consider cats therapy animals because they seem to do whatever they want instead of trying to please their humans, this cat was different. He was very attuned to my emotions, and each night in the bed that felt so empty since Skip passed, Webster would rest on my chest and purr until my sobs subsided and my breathing steadied, at which point he would move farther down the bed, often curling at

Webster posing on a shelf on the stair landing. After his death, I put a statue of a ginger cat in this same spot for comfort.

the small of my back, which was always cold without my heater man. Though the nightly sobbing stopped after a month or two, Webster's routine of purring on my chest as I relaxed into sleepiness persisted for the rest of his life with me. It was no longer daily, or even predictably regular, but it was always a delight when he would follow me upstairs to bed and settle on my chest for a few precious minutes of purring as I first eased into the pillows and turned out the light. And I would often wake to him curled at the small of my back in the morning. A good friend who knew both the cat and his namesake used to tell me that she believed Webster was channeling Skip.

During the pandemic isolation of 2020–2021, Webster also loved joining me in my Zoom yoga classes, where he would sit purring on my torso, sometimes during śavāsana, yoga's relaxation pose, and sometimes while I was in other poses as well. My instructor used to joke that he was doing her work for her since she could no longer come around the room to give her students the usual spinal presses she used to give in person for certain poses. Though Webster would sometimes lose interest before the pose was complete, he never actually left the room, and the instructor often saw his magnificent fluffy orange tail move across my screen while I was otherwise occupied in a long hold of the pose.

In the spring of 2021, when Webster turned fifteen years old, which is near the end of an indoor-only domestic cat's average life expectancy, I started to notice a distinct slowing on the part of my wonderful furboy. However much he slept during the day, though, he never tired of cuddling and purring, though he did start to get more scrawny. It was hard to tell when looking at him at a distance because of that beautiful long coat of his, but whenever I picked him up, I knew he was losing weight. And energy. Even so, I thought of it as inescapable aging, but it did start me worrying that when Webster passed on that it might trigger some kind of major grief eruption for me because he had been so tied in with my grief journey for the past ten years. When, as part of his annual check-up and bloodwork, the vet identified a heart-related problem developing, I started to worry.

So, I threw myself into all the research and planning for his care and impending end-of-life decisions in hopes that might lessen the inevitable blow when it came, even if it was months away. However, the situation intensified when further medical tests showed that Webster, the most loving and attentive cat I have ever owned, had a fatal tumor growing on his heart and didn't have much time left. Now we were talking days instead of months before the inevitable. Friends started to become concerned about me because they realized how much Webster had meant to me. I have always been attached to my pets, but this attachment was laden with echoes of my other grief as well. In hopes of avoiding a serious meltdown, I spent lots of energy on Webster's palliative care, even as his life force waned. No longer was he coming upstairs to the bedroom at night, but his purring was just as loud and soothing as ever whenever he crawled into my lap. It was almost a week before his euthanasia appointment that he had his final moments of lying on my legs in the recliner as we had done nearly every day for many years, and in his last few days he would only eat in small bites if I brought something to wherever he was resting, though he would still purr and lick my hands whenever I petted him. He seemed, all the way to the end, to be trying to take care of me, to "rise to the occasion" of pleasing me, as he had always done, and he never showed any of the obvious medical end-of-life symptoms I was reading about in the "how will I know when it's time" articles I found online, so I kept thinking things weren't quite at the end. Not just yet. In retrospect, I believe I should have taken him for euthanasia sooner than I did, though I imagine many pet owners make that same mistake because they are not ready to let go yet.

The expected meltdown didn't happen after all, and I believe it was because of two factors. First, I kept worrying about and planning for it (pre-grieving, in the jargon of grief counseling), so I was more prepared for it—fortified, if you will—against any surprise attacks. The second was the wonderful support I got from friends and family who understood just how much this animal meant to me and how closely our relationship was tied to my husband's death more than a decade before. Kensey and Tim brought their kids over for a sweet goodbye to Webster, and the whole family made sure I knew that both the cat and I were much loved. My wonderful neighbor (and Webster's "aunty" who cared for the cats whenever I was away) took me to the emergency clinic, where they did regular euthanasia procedures without an appointment, sitting next to me as Webster died peacefully in my arms; she also helped me bury him in my garden. And my delightful surrogate son, Zachary, who knew more than most about the intimate connections between Webster and Skip, called me for a long phone chat that evening, where we reminisced about each of them as he prepared for the same likely end coming soon for his sweet dog, Emmett, who had relationships with both of those loved ones we had lost.

Now, when I walk through my garden and see the place Webster is buried underneath the crabapple tree planted in Skip's memory when I first moved in, I feel an ache, but it's a manageable one, and the memory of my beautiful Webster continues to comfort me as he did in life.

Webster's final resting place by Skip's memorial tree.

PART THREE

FINDING MY WAY

CHAPTER THIRTEEN

REFLECTIONS ON WIDOWHOOD

THERE WAS NOTHING normal about this new normal for me, at least not in the first months and years after Skip's death. Everything in my life had been upended, and all I was trying to do was find a way to stay balanced and not fall into a hole of deep despair. One of the first things that changed for me was my relationship with certain friends. It turns out that in dealing with loss, I had two kinds of friends.

The first was the kind who said that said they wanted to help ("Call me any time, day or night, I'm here for you") but who never reached out in any meaningful way during those early months, instead waiting for me to take the initiative. But because I had no idea what I wanted or needed as I tried to move forward, perhaps due to the fog of widow brain or some remnants of the shock of deep grief, I could not reach out to them. So, they were never part of my resetting the boundaries and routines of this new life as a widow, and many of them drifted away over time, perhaps still waiting for me to call.

The second kind of friend was someone who, in the early weeks and months after Skip's death, just dropped by or sent an email or text at times to see if I wanted to join them for a walk or a trip to the store or a quick visit, always with no pressure. Even if I turned them down at first, these friends always extended themselves to me on a regular basis, waiting until I was ready to resume life as usual and making sure I knew they wanted to be part of it. These are the friends I have kept close all these years later.

Because of my academic nature and introverted tendencies, I started to read anything I could get my hands on about adjusting to life as a widow. Many of those things were spiritual in nature, but there was also some practical advice. Everything I read suggested in no uncertain terms that those who were newly widowed should not make any major changes immediately, no matter how tempting that might seem at first. I was still feeling uncertain of my place in a family I was just beginning to get to know and care for. And I had a job that I loved and wanted to keep; it was one place I was sure I belonged. So, I took that advice to heart and didn't make any significant changes in my living arrangements right away, though after a one-semester return to teaching in the spring, I did make a job change from teaching professor to a mid-level administrator. This turned out to be a godsend, because it moved me from a nine-month to a twelve-month contract, which accomplished two things: I was working year-round and no longer had summers off, which as a close friend had pointed out, would have been challenging without my gardening and travel partner, and in addition to raising my workload, it raised my annual salary by a third, enabling me to contemplate retiring a year before I had planned. So, I hunkered down in the home Skip and I had loved, embraced the memories that surrounded me, continued getting to know his family without him there to smooth the way, and waited for the right moment to make significant changes in my life.

During the first couple of years of my widowed life, the Stoughton family situation clarified for me. In some of the narratives I'd been reading, the road to maintaining relationships with the deceased spouse's family had been rough, especially when the widow/er was still relatively young. Because in the early days of our grieving, my stepdaughter had made a comment about me finding someone else, I was at first on edge about not being wanted, but over time, I realized that the comment had resulted from her fear that I might do just that. Others in my life wondered whether I was going to be interested in dating again, but I had lived alone for fifteen years before Skip came along, and I had watched my mother learn to live alone, appearing comfortable and content, for almost thirty-five years after my dad's death, so I made it clear that it would be a long time, if ever, before looking for a new partner would be a goal. I even started wearing both of our wedding rings (his re-sized to fit my much smaller fingers) and have continued to do so. Gradually, Kensey and I each worked through our fears and our grief, together and separately. Eventually, we developed a stable and loving relationship that was not dependent on me being part of a couple but being a member of the family in my own right. That relationship solidified about two years after Skip's death, when we began talking, in anticipation of my retirement, about looking for houses to buy, close to one another or with a mother-in-law dwelling attached. The words, "You're with us," during that search brought me enormous relief.

Between us, Skip and I had owned several properties in northern New York—we joked often about having a small real estate empire before we bought our house together—and had started selling properties before he died. Shortly after his death, I had to foreclose on an owner-held mortgage but was able to resell the property to a developer after a few months of harrowing uncertainty, especially without Skip's calming presence in the negotiations. I was able to sell our other properties when I was ready to retire and move to be nearer to the kids. It felt good but also bittersweet to divest myself of the remnants of our "empire," though it was an important step along my road forward. The most challenging aspect of all those real estate maneuvers was the fact of moving, which came just a few months shy of four years after his death. First, I had to pack up anything of Skip's that I thought others might like—his brother Mark got the vinyl collection, his nephew TJ got many of his slightly out-of-style but very nice banker's suits and dress shoes, Kensey got the kitchen items that had been used by her mother, including a set of stoneware dishes and the antique pickling crock—and tons of paper went to recycling. Skip was as much of a paperwork hoarder as I was, but no one wanted or needed much of it after his death, especially once the estate settled. Once all the giveaways had been accomplished, and a major garage sale took care of many of the household items I would no longer need in my smaller new house, I set out to pack the rest. I hit a serious snag because being alone while packing up the house threw me into regular grief eruptions that stopped my progress almost daily. I made the arrangements for a moving van, booked a flight for my son-in-law,

During the disruption of preparing to move house, Webster spent a lot of time hanging out on the piles of boxes, making sure I knew he was ready to go with me.

Tim, to northern New York so he could drive the van to Massachusetts, and arranged for moving help on the last day of the month. But when I was faced with needing to get everything left in our home into boxes for the move, I froze. I finally put out a call for help among my Facebook friends, something that was very hard for me to do, because many of them had commented on how impressed they were with my strength and ability to deal with my loss over the past few years.

To my surprise and delight, a number of helpers jumped into action to assist me in getting packed and ready in time to meet the real estate closing deadline. Some friends came for an hour here and there; one colleague I didn't know all that well but who lived nearby came several times for a couple hours at a time. And one former student drove from where he was living an hour away to help me pack my kitchen in one long afternoon. On the morning we were scheduled to pick up and load the truck, the folks at U-Haul tried to persuade me to accept a smaller truck than I had ordered, admitting they had screwed up the reservation

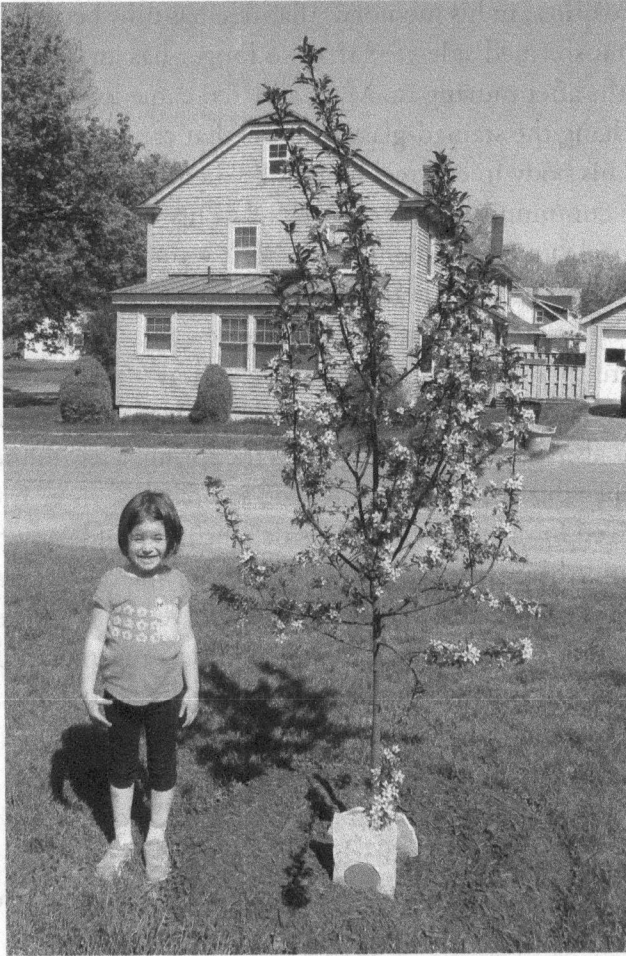

The memorial crabapple tree was planted in the side yard in the spring of 2015, with Maren's help to document the event.

and didn't have the truck I needed. My son-in-law was firm and direct with them. Skip would have approved, and though we had to drive to a different store, we did get the truck we needed. Once it was loaded and ready to go, we headed south to Massachusetts and my new life without Skip, leaving behind the home we had made together.

Once I unpacked all the boxes and deployed all the furniture, the first outdoor thing I did in my new home, a home Skip would never see but one I felt sure he would have approved of, was to plant a crabapple tree, one of his favorites, in his memory. That tree has now become the center-piece of a transformed side yard that no longer has any grass remaining. A few months after moving in, Mary and Ted came from the West Coast to help me hang the stained-glass window that created those prisms that had bathed his body in ethereal light as he died. It would have been easy in this new community to cocoon, to rely only on old friends at a distance and local family members, but I didn't want to do that, particularly because Skip had been such an outgoing and social person. I wanted to honor him by finding new friends for this new life.

One fortuitous thing that happened right away was I discovered that an actor friend I had enjoyed working with over twenty years ago in Portland, Oregon, was also moving to the region in the spring, a few months before I made the move that summer. I always had several close sister-friends wher-ever I had lived in the past, and it was delightful to find someone I could confide in and share with right away in this new place. Carmela's friend-ship has been an invaluable part of my ongoing recovery journey. She and her husband and I started having regular dinners together and exploring the local community. My first new affinity group, and one that I shared with my new/old friend, was associated with a small professional theatre company, similar to the one where we had worked together in Oregon. I had thought that I should start out in my new life by getting involved with the same creative activities that I had practiced throughout my career. It was familiar turf, a field where I was comfortable, and I enjoyed most of the people I worked with there; I even thought about taking a leadership position with the group. Further, by directing two plays with them, I was able to prove to myself that my creative mojo hadn't died with Skip. In the end, however, both my friend and I walked away from that company because of personal disagreements with management, though I remain proud of the work I did there. I didn't want to walk away from theatre entirely, though. I still had a script in the works that I'd been collaborating on with an old friend for many years and wanted to bring that to fruition, something I was able to experience more than a decade after Skip had participated in an early kitchen table read of the script's first draft.

But in addition to returning to familiar ground, I wanted—in fact, I craved—something creative I could do on my own, without needing the collaboration of others in such a significant way. So, I picked up a project I had started before Skip's death, when I was attempting to get promoted to full professor and started to think about it again. This time I focused only on the story I wanted to tell, not the promotion that might result from the project's success. Freed from the need to meet particular academic standards, I was able to start writing what publishers would call a human-interest story about my parents and their wartime experiences while my dad was in Europe during WWII, which I found much more fulfilling. Once that book was published, I focused on a memoir about how I had been able to find my genetic family members through DNA testing, something I had started a few years after Skip's death while still living in northern New York. To help with both endeavors, I found a writing group to support my newfound explorations outside of academia. That group of women writers has become important to me, both as individual good friends and as a safe and supportive place to test my new writing. In the years I've been attending, they have guided me through a total of three book manuscripts, including this one. As well, I started looking beyond theatre and writing folks to find other new friends. I discovered a book group associated with a local independent bookstore, and I've been reading with those women friends now for over six years. All of them are avid knitters, so I was able to rejuvenate my meager knitting skills for a time, until my eyesight started to fail. I also started getting to know the women in my small neighborhood, helping to start a quarterly neighborhood women's potluck to build some sense of community in our little development until COVID lockdown put an end to our gatherings.

Hanging out with and getting to know my grandchildren has been another important part of developing my new routines. They were just five months old and three years old when their "Papa" died, and as I write this, they are thirteen and sixteen. I see them often, and when they were younger they would spend extended periods of time at my house, sometimes right after school, sometimes when their parents needed to run errands on a weekend. They still come over for sleepovers now and then so their folks can get a date night and be able to sleep in the next morning. I often share memories of the Papa they barely knew, so he doesn't vanish from their lives altogether. Though I try not to communicate it to

Taken the second holiday season after Skip died, when the grandkids were still small enough for me to pick up both of them.

the kids, it makes me sad that he's missing what remarkable young people they are becoming.

So where does this leave me more than a decade after the sudden end of my previous life as a happily married woman and the beginning of being forced against my will into the unwanted role of widow? This life that I've built in the four years in northern New York and the almost ten years in western Massachusetts both includes and is separate from my life with Skip. Even so, I feel his presence often (or perhaps it's just my memory of him) in my new house, a house I've lived in longer than I lived with my husband. I've created new gardens that he would approve of, transforming the entire side lawn into a meadow beside a pollinator garden with that crabapple tree at its heart. Now I grow a few veggie plants to keep up his legacy, but most of the time I focus on the flowers and shrubs I love. I do my gardening alone, but sometimes I need help from my neighbor and fellow gardener, my son-in-law, or a local landscaping firm for the heavy projects that would have been Skip's.

I don't watch TV much anymore; it's not much fun without someone to share and unpack your programs with. My heart still lurches a bit when I change the sheets by myself, struggling with a task that was always more efficient with Skip's help. I cook for myself these days, though I rely often on prepared meals because cooking brings me little pleasure unless I'm doing it with my grandkids. In addition to the artwork that used to grace the walls of the house we shared, I've filled my shelves in the no-longer-so-new house with many images of that infamous geezer model who brought me such joy. I've heard that some widowed people don't want to see reminders of what they have lost because it brings them pain, but those images bring me regular comfort. In that, I have taken after my mother, who, after losing my dad suddenly in his late fifties, always loved to look at the slides he took of our family time together. As the photographer, he wasn't in many of the images, but it was how she experienced his presence. In spite of the fact that she never talked to me about her widowed experience, her actions and the fact that she lived a good life alone after Dad died became a kind of model for my own when the same thing happened to me.

There has been no dating nor any feeling that I need to find a new partner. When you've already had such a wonderful one, the memory is actually better than settling for second best in person. Those anniversaries that had been so intense and emotional during my early years as a widow (especially his birthday and death date, always so close together) are still marked, but are no longer days that stop my life in its tracks. In fact, they no longer require major rituals for me to get through them, though I always remember and pay some measure of attention to them. In warmer weather, I serve "Drinks on the Deck" for family or friends, something that Skip and I delighted doing in our home together, but instead of having the bartender serve us, I've learned to be the bartender in my own right. I think he would be proud of me.

And those prisms that have sustained me grace the walls in my dining room and kitchen on sunny days, and when they do, I greet them, speaking to them as if they were the spiritual embodiment of my lost love ("Hi, Babe, so glad you could come by today") and touching the patterns on the wall to feel their warmth on my skin, helping me remember

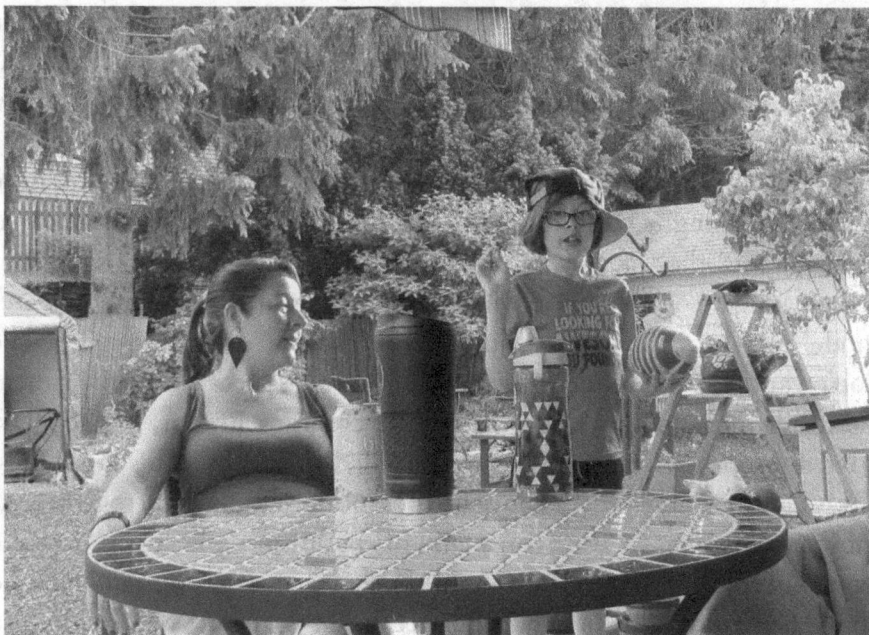

Views of a kid version of "Drinks on the Deck" with Kensey, Maren, and Trenton.

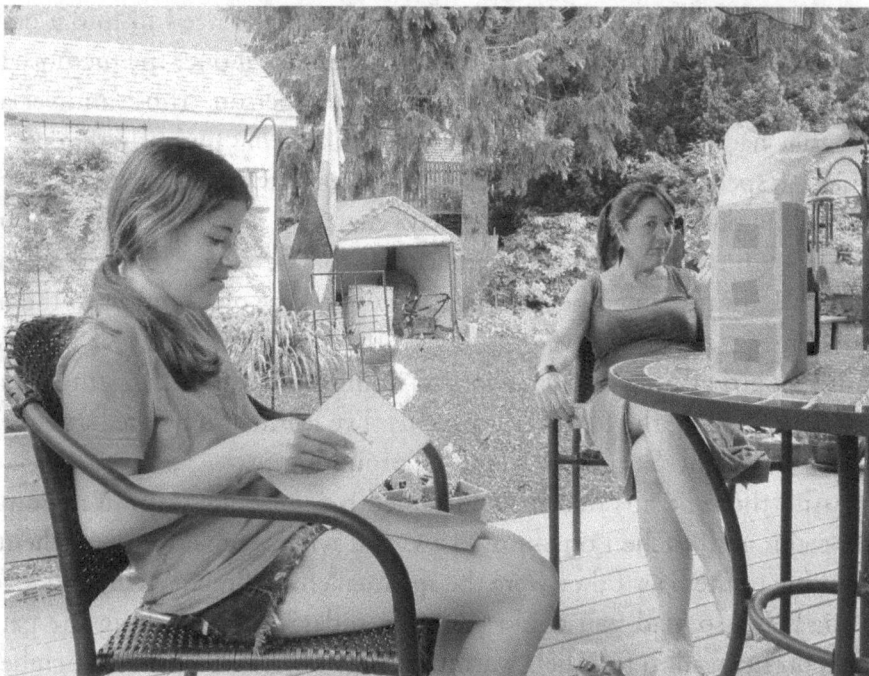

my "heater man." Whenever I wish Skip were here so I could consult him about business or financial matters, I pour myself a Manhattan, his favorite cocktail (counting out those ten ice cubes and intoning in my head as I end the count, "I lost my love on the ninth day of the tenth month"). Then I imagine what he might say to me about whatever it is that's troubling or confounding me. In the thirteen-plus years since his death, I have finally made peace with my initial worries about the complexities of reunion in the afterlife. I realize that I have been experiencing an afterlife of my own: a life without him beside me but with memories of our time together to sustain me. And I have survived. By the time I get to the other side, I suspect the issue will be moot. Is all this normal? Have I found for myself that mythical new normal each widow seeks? Who knows for sure? But it works for me.

AFTERWORD

DEAR SKIP: FINISHING A BOOK ABOUT LOVE AND LOSS
April 18, 2022
(Eleven years and six months after)

Dear One,

Though I haven't written in my grief journal for over a decade, I thought it appropriate to make one last entry to you as I complete the manuscript of my grief memoir, which I'm calling *That Day and What Came After: Finding and Losing the Love of My Life in Six Short Years.* It's now been more years that I've been your widow than the time we had together in this lifetime. Once I found some semblance of a normal existence on my own after your death, it took me several years to start writing about our life together, especially about that day I lost you. In fact, I think it was at least five years before I got serious about doing it and even longer before what I wrote was anything more than maudlin self-pity and continued breast-beating over my loss. I stopped the regular grief journaling about six months after you died, but I have never stopped thinking about you every day.

When I thought about what it was like to write my story, I recalled a poem a widow-friend posted to Facebook recently about love and loss that resonated with me. The basic premise was that there is no single moment when you lose a loved one, especially an intimate partner or spouse. Instead, after that first earth-shattering loss, you continue to lose

This is the last photo I ever took of Skip, a few days before he died. He wasn't happy because he had discovered our vandalized car in our own driveway.

them in different ways every day for the rest of your life. That's the way it is for me. I lose you in small moments during the day that I can no longer share with you. I lose you in often unused items that used to be yours but that I can't allow myself to get rid of, like your favorite sweatshirt that I wore every day during the first month after your death and have worn often in cooler weather ever since. I lose you in actions or routines we used to do together, things like changing the sheets or working in the garden. I lose you in special moments we used to enjoy together, especially walking the yard making plans or Drinks on the Deck after an afternoon of gardening. I lose you in words unspoken or remembered as I watch our grandchildren grow, remembering how much you adored them and how much I wish you could see them maturing and changing as the years fly by.

Though these moments of loss no longer hijack me with emotional meltdowns almost twelve years after your death, I have not ceased to feel them, only learned to manage their emotional impact. They range from the mundane (I do a Jumble puzzle every day in the newspaper, just as we always did, and I think of you when I'm stumped and frustrated and feel like giving up—a feeling you refused to give in to, even if the puzzle took you all day to complete), to the major (I talk every large decision over with you—whether it's about house or garden planning or large financial matters—often in my head but sometimes even out loud or with a drink to soothe me), and everything in-between. Not a day goes by that I don't wish you were still here, but I have learned to live without your physical presence. I couldn't do it without the remarkable memories we made together, and while I don't spend all my time thinking about the past, those memories do help me appreciate what a blessing you were in my life.

I feel your loss most whenever I have a late afternoon drink on the deck while enjoying the gardens without you, whenever I watch Maren and Trenton doing just about anything, whenever I travel (which isn't often anymore), whenever we hit the holidays, especially the time frame between your birthday in early November and the New Year, and whenever I'm almost asleep at night, missing the warmth of your body curling around me. I feel your presence with me in the house whenever the prismatic light appears on the walls in the dining room and kitchen, and I feel your presence in the yard whenever I'm working with the plants, digging in the dirt, or even just sitting in the sun surveying my peaceful surroundings with pleasure. Feeling your loss and feeling your presence have become entwined in my emotional life, though that entanglement no longer derails my psyche. It's become part of my reality.

Writing this book has helped me share you with so many people, especially those I would have loved for you to meet if you had moved with me to western Massachusetts to be near the kids and grandkids. The women in my writing group have enjoyed getting to know you (one even called it "falling in love" with you) through listening to my chapter drafts, and one of the women in my spiritual circle insists that she sees Stoughton trucks whenever she travels to the regular art shows she and her painter husband attend each year. She calls those sightings "messages from Spirit," letting me know through her that you are still watching out for me. And I wonder, why don't you appear to me in the same

This photo, taken on our vacation in Maine, is one of my favorites. It lives on a bookshelf in my living room so I can see it every day.

way? Then I realize that you and many of our friends saw me as a strong person, able to handle just about anything, so perhaps you believe I don't need you anymore. It's true that I have been muddling through without you, but that is because I was forced by circumstance to learn how to do so in order to survive your death. It doesn't mean I don't wish every day that things were different and that you were still here with me.

So now, as I approach the end of this memoir, I worry that I will lose you all over again when I stop writing about our life together. I may lose you each day in ways large and small, and yet I will never lose the sense of love and gratitude for having known you in this lifetime, even as I continue to reinvent my life anew each day in the supposed "new normal" that seems straightforward in theory but often elusive in reality.

ABOUT THE AUTHOR

Rebecca Daniels (MFA, PhD) taught performance, writing, and speaking in liberal arts universities for over twenty-five years, including St. Lawrence University in Canton, New York, from 1992–2015. She was the founding producing director of Artists Repertory Theatre in Portland, Oregon, directed with many professional Portland theatre companies in the 1980s, and is the author of the groundbreaking *Women Stage Directors Speak: Exploring the Effects of Gender on Their Work* (McFarland, 1996, 2000) and has been published in multiple professional theatre journals.

After her retirement from teaching, she turned her focus to creative nonfiction and began her association with Sunbury Press with *Keeping the Lights on for Ike: Daily Life of a Utilities Engineer at AFHQ in Europe During WWII; or, What to Say in Letters Home When You're Not Allowed to Write about the War* (2019), a book based on her father's letters home from Europe during WWII.

Her second book with Sunbury, *Finding Sisters: How One Adoptee Used DNA Testing and Determination to Uncover Family Secrets and Find Her Birth Family* (2021), explores how DNA testing, combined with traditional genealogical research, helped her find her genetic parents, two half-sisters, and other relatives in spite of being given up for a closed adoption at birth.

Learn more at rebecca-daniels.com.

www.ingramcontent.com/pod-product-compliance
Lightning Source LLC
Chambersburg PA
CBHW010856090426
42737CB00020B/3395